BETWIXT MOOR AND

Cover: Simon Jones climbing stile at 726565; see Walk 8

Stone slab stile

BETWIXT MOOR AND SEA

South Devon Rambles

Roger Jones

Illustrations by Simon Jones

EX LIBRIS PRESS

First published 1987
Ex Libris Press
1 The Shambles
Bradford on Avon
Wiltshire

Typeset in 11 on 13 point Plantin
by Saxon Printing Ltd., Derby

ISBN 0 948578 07 6

Other Books by Roger Jones:

A Book of Newton Abbot
Where Wiltshire Meets Somerset
Wiltshire Rambles
Down the Bristol Avon
Green Road to Land's End

Edited and Introduced by Roger Jones:

The Walker's Companion
West Country Tour

Printed in Great Britain by A. Wheaton & Co. Ltd., Exeter

CONTENTS

Wooden step stile

PREFACE

I lived in South Devon for four years, from 1976 until 1980. As a stranger from south-east England I was naturally curious to explore these very different surroundings. June was the month of my arrival: the beginning of that unprecedentedly long, hot and dry summer of 1976. I had been appointed Divisional Librarian at Newton Abbot and, before my family and I were able to move into our new house in the town, I decided to take advantage of the glorious weather and save the money that would have been spent on board and lodgings by pitching my tent on a farm camping site at Daccombe, on the Newton Abbot side of Torquay. It was in this holiday mood that my four year stint at Newton Abbot began.

Quite soon I fell to boasting to my friends up-country that Newton Abbot was an ideal place to live, being about equidistant from Dartmoor National Park in one direction and the sandy beaches at Teignmouth and Dawlish in the other, and only about 15 minutes drive from each. How many times that first summer did we all enjoy a drive to the beach for a cooling evening swim, with perhaps a stop at some village pub for a drink on the way home. The children thought they were having an extended holiday and, after three months of hot sunshine and regular expeditions, I had much the same feeling myself.

Later, on my days off, I took the opportunity to explore Newton Abbot, which seemed to be a town unfairly neglected, and even abused, by writers of books on Devon. The coast path from the Teign estuary down and around to the Plym I found full of interest and, for much of its length, a spectacular walking experience. The countryside immediately around Newton Abbot attracted me for its interest too, but also for its accessibility.

I discovered the Pathfinder maps of the Ordnance Survey and spent hours poring over them, in particular tracing the green-dashed rights of way through fields and woods and along tracks and towpaths. This armchair activity I found almost as enjoyable as the walking itself. And yet there are always surprises to be found en route which are not apparent on the maps and, of course, the beauty and charm of the Devon countryside can only be truly appreciated using Shanks's pony. Surprisingly perhaps, the wide open spaces of Dartmoor did not especially attract me. To begin my walking career I preferred the gentle hills and combes of South Devon with all their reminders of human settlement over the centuries.

After moving to West Wiltshire in 1980 I found myself regularly drawn back to Devon, usually on business, but always ready to mix that activity with a little pleasure in the form of a brief ramble. I had found the South Hams beyond Totnes an area of particular delight and now returned to walk more of its green lanes and to seek out ways beside its unique drowned valleys.

In setting down these circular rambles I hope others will be more able to share the pleasure of walking in a quiet and still largely unspoilt corner of England away from, if not the madding crowd, at least certain rather more popular destinations on Dartmoor and the coast.

Roger Jones
1987

INTRODUCTION

Where is South Devon?

South Devon is generally reckoned to be that part of Devon to the south of Dartmoor which stretches from the River Exe (or sometimes the Teign) to the Tamar. This includes the South Hams which itself refers to the narrower wedge of land between the Teign (sometimes the Dart) and the Plym, which latter definition more or less corresponds with the present-day District Authority of that name.

Torbay, which includes Torquay, Paignton and Brixham, is by far the biggest built-up area in South Devon; the coast here certainly attracts the rambler as well as everybody else who visits these towns but the burgeoning estates inland hardly do so and the entire conurbation is omitted in the pages of this book, as is Plymouth in the far west. Much more characteristic of South Devon which, apart from Torbay and Plymouth, is essentially a rural landscape, are the small towns of Totnes and Kingsbridge and the old port of Dartmouth.

South Devon is one of the most universally hilly parts of England. The constant upping and downing lends any walker an ever-changing scene – there are almost no straight roads. Valleys and hills wrinkle the landscape in haphazard fashion – there seems to be little pattern. It is of course true that the major rivers of this well-watered land descend and radiate from the hub of Dartmoor like the spokes of a wheel – Teign, Dart, Avon, Erme, Yealm and Plym – but the rivers themselves twist and turn and, more significantly, their tributary streams in the hinterland of South Devon often follow sinuous courses between interlocking hillsides.

And what hillsides! Having grown accustomed to the south-east of England, I always expect hills to rise gently and then give way rather more suddenly to the softer rocks beneath in the form of an escarpment: a gradual incline to an edge above a concavity. The hills of South Devon are, I find, never concave. Because they are so prolific and so jumbled together they all seem to be vying to assert themselves 'fat side out' – slopes here are most definitely convex, a characteristic which has led more than one writer to describe the lansdcape as 'billowy'.

This is a warm, fat land. The climate is the kindest in Britain. Adequate rains, numerous rivers, more sunshine, clean air blowing in from the ocean on predominantly south-westerly winds; and the estuaries – those fingers of the sea which reach up into the heart of South Devon to carry with them a warming marine influence – all this contributes to the far-famed fertility and attractiveness of South Devon.

Geology

The basic determinant of any landscape is its underlying geology, the story of the rocks beneath. There are many kinds of rocks representing different geological ages to be found in South Devon. This succession of strata does not form a neat layered cake but has been subject to folding and faulting, sometimes extreme, sometimes more gentle, in the earth's crust. The picture is further complicated by the effects of aerial and marine erosion. This basis of geology and weathering, together with the impact of human settlement, adds up to the landscape we see today, in all its dazzling variety.

The red rocks which most people associate with Devon in fact cover only about a quarter of the county. This is the New Red Sandstone of the Permian Period and follows the coast from Exmouth, with a minor interruption north of Torquay, to reach Torbay. This formation, consisting of wind- and water-borne sandstones and breccias formed in semi-arid conditions, contains fragments of rocks formed in earlier times. These include the granite of Dartmoor, dating from the Carboniferous Period but having no connection with the Coal Measures which we usually associate with that time. The Dartmoor granite, like the granite outcrops further west in Cornwall, is an igneous rock formed deep in the earth's crust which cooled and solidified slowly to give shape to its massive crystalline structure.

This granite intrusion, now exposed and comprising the Dartmoor upland, forms the natural northern boundary of South Devon. Fragments of Devonian limestone are also found in the New Red Sandstone formation, the same limestone to be found in the hills and cliffs around Torquay, at Berry Head, to the south-east of Newton Abbot and in the west around Plymouth. This stone varies in colour – it is usually light or dark grey and veined with white calcite – often coral-bearing, the coral cross-sections showing up in the ashlar blocks which were a favourite building material in Victorian Torquay and Newton Abbot and many of the villages roundabout. All the local quarries are now gone but one very large one is worked at Stoneycombe near Kingskerswell. This place yields a distinctive pink limestone which is to be found in new garden walls all over South Devon, even many miles from its place of origin.

Older than the Devonian limestone is a great thickness of strata containing beds of slate and sandstone, often interspersed with volcanic rocks. These formations also belong to the Devonian Period. Devon is the only county to lend its name to a period of geological history – rocks of this period and the fossils which geologists need to identify properly the succession of beds are well represented in the county. Shales, later compacted into slates, were deposited as a sediment under the sea, this gentle process of accumulation at times disturbed by submarine volcanic eruptions which resulted in lava spreading on the sea floor. Sometimes, too, molten rock intruded itself amongst the layers of sediment as walls (known as dykes) and sheets (sills). Such local intrusions quickly cooled to form rocks like dolerite. These

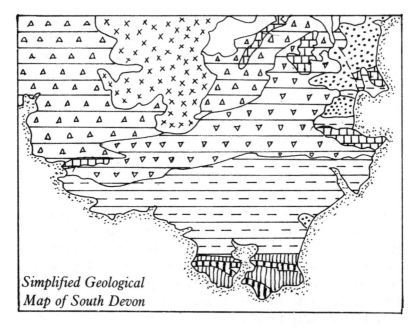

Simplified Geological
Map of South Devon

Key:

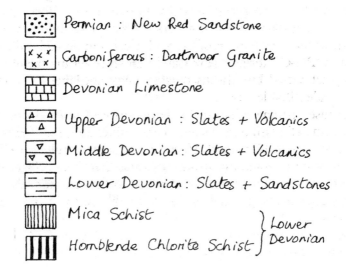

Permian : New Red Sandstone

Carboniferous : Dartmoor Granite

Devonian Limestone

Upper Devonian : Slates + Volcanics

Middle Devonian : Slates + Volcanics

Lower Devonian : Slates + Sandstones

Mica Schist

Hornblende Chlorite Schist } Lower Devonian

fine crystalline rocks make good, tough roadstone; dolerite is excavated as such at Tor Quarry near Kingsbridge.

These varied formations of the Middle and Lower Devonian compose the bulk of the land of South Devon. They are perhaps most typified by the slatey rocks which make up so much of the coastal scenery from Plymouth to Hope Cove and Dartmouth to Sharkham Point. These slates can be very beautiful – often so contorted that they appear to be stacked at all angles, exhibiting colours ever-changing through shades of red, green, yellow and brown and cleaving as thinly as a pack of cards, the faces of each piece shiny and lustrous.

The southernmost part of South Devon, and that part of the coast with the most spectacular scenery, lies between Bolt Head and Bolt Tail to the west of the Kingsbridge estuary and between Portlemouth Down and Start Point to the east. These rugged cliffs and the immediate hinterland are separated from the main body of South Devon by a fault line, known as the Start Boundary, running east/west.

The rocks here are known as schists and are termed metamorphic, that is, rocks whose structure have been changed by the effects of heat and pressure whilst buried deep in the earth's crust. Old geological maps generally cast these metamorphic schists at the very bottom of the geological column and indicate them as 'Pre-Cambrian?', Pre-Cambrian representing the oldest geological period but also used as a convenient label for otherwise unidentifiable strata.

Because metamorphic rocks have changed their form so drastically, all fossil remains have been obliterated, thus making identification problematical. However, recent research, especially that using radiometric dating, indicates that these schists are around 300 million years old. This suggests that they are of Lower Devonian age, like the strata to the north of the Start Boundary.

The schists are of two types: the mica schists and hornblende-chlorite schists, according to the preponderance of those particular minerals. Both are rather slatey in appearance, the former smooth and with a silvery sheen (from the mica), the latter more massive with a green coloration (from the chlorite). The sound of the word 'schist' seems to capture the character of the mica variety very well. Veins of white quartz, or milkstone, are often found interspersed with these two types of schist.

The geology of South Devon comes to life along the coast where the sea conveniently provides cross-sections for our inspection and the county thus provides many classic geological sites. There are not so many opportunities inland, except in old quarries – which are many, but not always beside rights of way. There are cuttings for roads – there are some attractive sections along the A38 on the way to Plymouth – as well as more modest exposures on the flanks of old sunken lanes. Yet there is one outstanding opportunity of viewing the local stone and that is in the buildings; generally speaking, the older the building, the more likely it is to be built of local stone.

People in the Landscape

The original Celtic inhabitants of Devon became known as the Damnonians, a name derived from the Celtic word *dun* , a hill, so that the Damnonians were known as the hilltop dwellers. The ancient kingdom of Damnonia once extended from Cornwall to Hampshire, but then contracted into Dyfnaint (hence Devon), meaning the land of the deep, dark combes, and more or less corresponded with the Devon we know today, comprising that south-west portion of England from the Tamar to the Axe.

The meanings of both ancient names suggest that Devon was a thickly wooded region and that human settlement was pretty much restricted to the open hilltops. Evidence of Celtic fortifications dating from pre-Roman times and guarding the most vulnerable approaches can be found, for example, at Castle Hill in Dartmouth and on Milber Down outside Newton Abbot. The Celtic *dun*, was later supplanted by the Saxon word *bury*. Hence, for example, the place name Denbury, a village between Newton Abbot and Totnes near which there is an ancient earthwork atop a wooded eminence. It is believed that, at this site, the natives resisted the Saxon advance, *Den* referring to the Dumnonians. The Romans occupied Britain for some four centuries but they did not colonise the land much further west than Exeter (although there is evidence that the Romans established a presence on Milber Down). Thus it was not until the eighth century and the gradual movement west of the Saxons that the Damnonians were pushed across the Tamar into Cornwall.

The Saxons were above all farming folk and during the following centuries the descendants of these pioneering people gradually changed the face of the landscape. They put down deep roots in building their farms, their churches and villages. They built in wood rather than stone so that practically nothing tangible remains of their presence. Nothing, that is, save the place names they bequeathed, and the basic pattern of fields and hedgerows which largely survives to this day. The settlement of the countryside continued in Norman times, and the network of hedgerows was further extended during the Enclosure Movement, when the great open fields and much of the common land was requisitioned for use with new farming methods, though South Devon was probably less affected than other parts of England at this time. The antiquity of the hedge system is proved by the frequent occurrence of the suffix, *hay, haye*, or *hayne*, meaning hedged enclosure. As the woods were felled the hedge system was established to enclose the largest intakes and many of these great hedgebanks denoted a boundary of ownership as well as quite often forming a parish boundary.

Sometimes the hedge comprised one line of growth on a single bank; sometimes it formed a double line with a cart track between. The many twists and turns of some hedgerows indicate that an obstable, such as a rock or a large tree, presented itself to the hedger. Inspection of a Pathfinder map or observation in the field reveals that valleys were more irregularly hedged than the naturally less congested higher ground. This shows that the higher ground was first taken in and upon the largest scale. Such woodland as remains in South Devon, and there is rather little, especially in the fertile South Hams district, tends to be concentrated in the valleys or on the sides of hills too steep to be effectively worked as arable land. Today our farmers produce more food than we need and, at the time of writing, the government is considering ways to take land out of food production and back to timber. It will be interesting, in years to come, to see how effective such measures prove.

Saxon settlement began in the sixth century and gradually spread during the next two hundred years. Devon formed part of the Saxon Kingdom of Wessex and was alone in resisting the incursions of the warring Danes: Exeter was fought over for some 130 years, the Danes finally being repelled in 1003.

Yet neither Devon nor any part of the Kingdom could deny the victory of the Normans, with their superior arms and organisation, in the eleventh century. As elsewhere in England, the Normans assumed ownership and control of the land but without necessarily much affecting the activities of the countryside; their undeniable presence is evidenced in their great castles and manor houses, their churches and monasteries. The Normans built not casually in wood but monumentally in stone, and such edifices became an enduring tribute to their power and authority.

Perhaps Devon's Golden Age, and particularly South Devon's, was the Elizabethan period of seafaring. Many Devon men won distinction in their pioneering voyages of discovery and settlement. Sir Humphrey Gilbert left Dartmouth upon a colonising expedition to the New World and laid claim to Newfoundland in 1579. Dartmouth was the birthplace of the Navy but most voyages set sail from Plymouth. It was from here that Sir Francis Drake set off to defeat the Spanish Armada. Less glorious, but perhaps even more glamorous, were the large numbers of pirates, privateers and smugglers who worked out of

South Devon.

Yet apart from this famous interlude, Devon has remained a quiet and, in comparison with much of Britain, a predominantly rural county. And because the south-west peninsula is geographically cut off from the rest of the country, Devon has not usually played a significant role in the great events which have stirred the rest of the country. It has been said that the history of Exeter is the history of Devon and, certainly, the county town has been fought over on many occasions and the outcome for Exeter has determined the outcome for Devon. Exeter surrendered to William the Conqueror in 1068 after an 18 day siege when William set to restoring the city as a fortress. The county town was besieged in the Wars of the Roses and during the Civil Wars. The Duke of Monmouth landed at Brixham in 1688 but scarcely saw any action in Devon before moving into Somerset.

Thus it was that Devon survived and indeed prospered, depending largely upon its agriculture, and building what industries it did very much upon its agricultural base. The Cistercian monks of Buckfast Abbey introduced the first sheep to Devon c. 1148. Buckfast means 'deer fastness' and leigh means pasturage. Here the monks had access to an extensive grazing area, once occupied by deer and now, increasingly, by sheep. They thereby laid the basis of the wool industry, both within the county and by means of a profitable export trade. Cloth later began to be produced in the county, the numerous rivers giving power to the mills employed in its manufacture, as they had to the fulling mills. Totnes, Modbury and Newton Bushel later became thriving centres of the wool industry, the finished cloth being exported from Exeter via Topsham. As the age of the factory and the steam engine progressed the trade was gradually lost to the newly industrialised regions of Britain. Devon may have lost its manufacturing capacity, but the demand for wool from the county's sheep was still high and sheep farmers maintained their living.

Agriculture remains by far Devon's most important industry.

Because of the lie of the land, arable crops are not of great importance, although quantities of cereals and root crops are grown. Farming is in fact very mixed, with dairy cattle, beef cattle, sheep rearing, arable crops and market gardening all sharing in the lasting importance of Devon, and especially fertile South Devon, as a premier farming district.

The hilly nature of the landscape has encouraged this mixed agriculture, with farmers fitting their crops to suit their particular needs. One happy result of this diversity is that hedges and tracks, though some have undoubtedly been lost, are still very much a feature of the region and, along with those hedges and tracks, many miles of rights of way have been retained. Although relatively thinly populated outside of Torbay and Plymouth, South Devon, like the rest of the county, has a dense and intricate network of lanes, though many are deeply sunken and just wide enough for one vehicle to proceed with care. In addition to the metalled roads are many unmade tracks between high hedgebanks. Since the advent of motorised transport, many of these tracks (or 'throats' as they have been known locally) have fallen into disuse and become completely overgrown, even if they have been lucky enough to escape having their ends sealed by the indiscriminate dumping of rubbish. In such cases rights of way have sometimes been lost, though in others field paths running parallel to the old tracks have been established as a substitute route for pedestrians.

It must be said that local authorities, particularly South Hams District Council and some of the parish councils, are taking an increasing interest in their rights of way and signposting has much improved in recent years. A scheme funded by the Manpower Services Commission began in 1983 to research, survey and maintain green lanes in Devon. Its manager for the first two years was Valerie Belsey of Dartington who opened the Green Lanes Centre in April 1987. This Centre offers guided walks, holidays and publications and is ultimately aimed at the preservation – through knowledge and use – of local green lanes.

The deeply sunken aspect of many Devon lanes has long been recognised as a characteristic of the county. Some curious explanations for this phenomenon have been advanced. One I came across in an old book (*From John O'Groats to Land's End* : Caxton, 1916) was given by a native upon enquiry by the author, John Naylor: 'We asked why the lanes in Devonshire are so much below the surface of the land, and he said they had been constructed that way in very ancient times to hide the passage of cattle and produce belonging to the British from the sight of their Saxon oppressors.'

The true explanation must surely by more prosaic. In constructing the ways, attempts would naturally have been made to level out the steep gradients by digging into the peaks. The passage of feet and hooves and wheels would, over the years, have worn down the surface and rains would have washed out any loose material which accumulated. Today many unmade tracks have worn down to the bedrock, all the soil and sub-soil having been prised loose and, after rain, become fast flowing streams.

Hedgebanks, fieldpaths, boundary paths, farm tracks, green roads, sunken lanes; all these provide the walker, where rights of way exist, with opportunities to view the rural hinterland of South Devon from a variety of vantage points. To walk these old ways is to follow in the footsteps of folk from the Saxon era onwards, be they the footsteps of farm labourers, packhorses carrying wool to the mill or to market, or the lord of the manor on horseback surveying his estate. Follow these ways and you will not only enjoy the best views in South Devon but will also sense history all around you.

Place Names

The place names of South Devon make an interesting study, as they do anywhere in England. Almost all the village and town names are derived from Old English roots, a fact which surely indicates that South Devon was widely settled by the Saxons. Only the river names reveal British, or Celtic, origins – not perhaps surprising, when one remembers that the rivers were here long before any permanent settlements.

Avon, of course, is a common river name in southern and western England and is derived from the British *abona* meaning water or stream. Teign is a British root meaning simply stream and Lemon, a tributary of the Teign which flows through Newton Abbot, is derived from elm. I had always assumed that the River Dart was so named because it flowed swift as a dart. In fact the word comes from the British for oak.

The naming of the River Erme is more problematical; some authorities indicate that Erme could be a Celtic river name, others that the river name is derived from the Old English *Iermen-tun*, or chief tun (or farm). Similarly, the naming of the River Plym is derived from the settlement of Plymstock, meaning the stoke (or place) where plum trees grow. Other Stokes include Stoke Fleming, where the manor was held by William le Fleming in 1219, Stoke Gabriel on the opposite bank of the Dart Estuary, where the church has a joint dedication to St Mary and St Gabriel, and Stokenham: 'the Stoke in low-lying river land'.

The remaining place names in South Devon are of Old English origin and can be divided into those which derive their appellation from persons and those from features of topography or natural history, or both. Hence:

Named after persons and natural features:
Aveton Gifford and *Blackawton* are both derived from 'Afa's tun', the latter Black to distinguish it. Only later (in 1242) did Walter Giffard hold the manor.
Dittisham – Dyddi's Ham
Ipplepen – Ipela's pen (or fold)
Loddiswell – Lod's Spring (well)
Torbryan – hill (tor) held by Wydo de Brianne
Totnes – Totta's Ness (or headland)

Named after features of topography or natural history:
Diptford – deep ford
Frogmore – frog lake or pool
Harberton – tun on the gentle stream
Marldon – hill overgrown with gentian (meargella)
Ringmore – reedy moor
Slapton – tun by the slaep (miry place)
Thurlestone – stone with a hole (named after Thurlestone Rock)

The origins of some place names are dubious; Ashprington may refer to the tun on ash hill, or may be derived from a personal name. Similarly, Malborough may mean 'Maerla's Hill' or 'hill where grow gentians (maergella)'. Buckland is a common Devon place name and means 'land held by charter'. The root word Burg or Bury means fortified place and is found in Berry Pomeroy – the burg held by Radulf de Pomerei (1086), Denbury – the burg of the Devon people, ie. the British natives, and Modbury – the burg where moots are held. North Huish points up another aspect of social history long forgotten: Old English 'hiwisc' meant household or hide, a hide being a measure of land which would support one family and its dependants.

The meanings of place names are not always easy to unravel, nor can we ever be certain of the origins of some. Those of South Devon form a stark contrast to the names further west, on the far side of Plymouth where the British were driven back by the colonising Saxons and where place names reflect Cornwall's survival as a refuge of the Celts.

THE WALKS

The sketch maps provided, together with the detailed descriptions of the routes, should be sufficient guidance for the intending walker. Nevertheless, the corresponding Ordnance Survey map is always a useful companion.

All 15 walks here are included within the scope of the 1:50,000 Landranger 202 map: Torbay and South Dartmoor area. This map shows all rights of way in red ink.

The 1:25,000 scale maps are the best for planning walks. In 1986 South Devon became number 20 in the Ordnance Survey Leisure Map series. This includes the Dart and Kingsbridge Estuaries and the hinterland between – covering Walks 4-12 in this book. This, the relevant Pathfinder or other 1:25,000 O.S. map is indicated at the beginning of each walk. The map reference refers to the starting point.

The routes vary from 2½ to 6 miles in length – none are over-strenuous and most are well waymarked and provided with stiles at crossing points. The only possible problem is mud. It must be said that the rich soil of hilly South Devon is likely to be muddy, especially along low-lying and enclosed paths, in all but the driest of times. Boots or stout shoes are therefore recommended.

Key to maps :

～～ lane or road

_ _ _ _ track

········ footpath

↗ stream or river
(arrow shows direction of flow)

WALK 1   NEWTON ABBOT

via Bradley Woods, West Ogwell and East Ogwell

Map: Newton Abbot Sheet SX 87/97

Map Reference: 853709

Distance: 5½ miles

This walk follows the valley of the River Lemon upstream through Bradley Woods, justly renowned as a local beauty spot and worth the stranger's notice. Entry to the woods is guarded by Bradley Manor, a truly delightful house dating from the fourteenth century and now owned by the National Trust. Chercombe Bridge marks the end of the woods but the route follows the Lemon further upstream before crossing that river and heading up a tributary valley by field paths to reach West Ogwell, a settlement consisting of a redundant church, a convent and a farm.

From West Ogwell the route follows quiet lanes, with a distant view to Channings Wood Prison, to reach the much larger and still expanding village of East Ogwell; here there is a pub – the Jolly Sailor. Rights of way are followed to return to Bradley Woods and a path along the south bank of the Lemon.

The starting point of this walk is reached from the **Totnes Road** by leaving Newton Abbot and turning right along **Steps Meadow**, beside Baker's Park. At the bottom there is a car park.

From here head across the bottom of the field to reach a bridge over the River Lemon, and very shortly a second bridge where you pass a notice indicating that the grounds belong to the National Trust. You can see the white gabled front of **Bradley Manor** beyond the gates ahead.

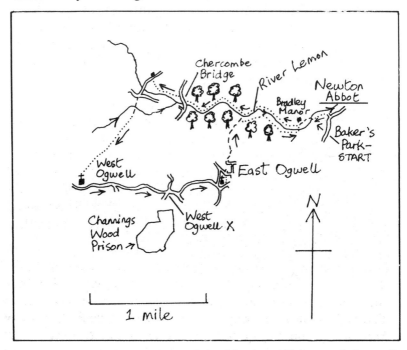

Bear left and follow the path beside the mill leat and the wall of the Manor grounds on your right. The open meadow on your left narrows to a point where there is a bridge across the river. This bridge will be reached on the final leg of the walk back from East Ogwell. To follow the river upstream take the path on the right bank. This leads you through riverside woods and is enjoyable in all seasons. After about half a mile a weir is reached; it is at this point that the channel of water was diverted to serve the many wool and leather mills along Bradley Lane in Newton Abbot, and which still flows as far as Bradley Manor.

Just past the weir you cross a stile to enter an open field; follow the path to the bridge by the former Ogwell Mill. This boggy field is a good place to see marsh marigold and lady's smock in the spring and summer. The track leading up from the ford beside the bridge on the opposite bank leads to East Ogwell. However, continue the walk by passing through the kissing gate by the pedestrian bridge and follow the right hand bank of the Lemon. Once past the meadow you cross a stile to re-enter the woods. Notice a number of lime kilns beside the path with their attendant quarries behind.

At the end of the woods you reach a gate with the instructions Please Close Gate. The right of way passes through the garden of the house ahead. Exit here by a gate; Chercombe Bridge is to your left. Do not cross the bridge but bear right for a few yards and look out for a stile in the hedgerow opposite. Cross here and follow the right of way straight ahead with the river on your left. Cross the stile in the far corner and follow the river to reach a gap in the far corner; now head for the white-painted cottage by a stile beside a gate in the far corner.

Bear left along the lane to cross the river. Climb up to the T-junction and bear left. Very shortly on the right look out for three gates – take the centre one which is indicated Public Footpath. Follow this way between hedges. Beyond the muddy bottom you climb again towards a gate. About 25 yards below bear right through a gap between an ash and an oak tree. Now bear left and follow the hedgebank on the left.

Over the brow of the hill can be seen a stile at a point about 50 yards to the right of the far left corner. Cross the middle of the next sloping field to a gate on the opposite side; now follow the left-hand hedgerow to reach another gate beneath a row of stately horse chestnut trees. Head down slightly to a gate in the barbed wire fence. As you approach the gate you can see the tower of **West Ogwell church** ahead. On the left is the convent which, approached from this angle, looks most undistinguished.

Later you will see the belfry and the drive up to the classical frontage.

Carry on to cross the stile just to the right of the church tower; this leads you into the churchyard. After visiting the church, which is generally kept unlocked, follow the lane past the convent and due east towards East Ogwell. You can see, from the lane looking south, the wooded eminence of Denbury Camp (past West Ogwell Farm, there is an indicated footpath across fields to Denbury). A little further on appears the high boundary fence of Channings Wood Prison and the former Army huts which comprise much of its accommodation. You may also spot a lime kiln beside the lane before reaching **West Ogwell Cross**.

Continue straight on for **East Ogwell**. You enter the village at a T-junction where you turn right and then bear left past the Old Manor House, the Jolly Sailor pub and left into the church. Follow the footpath through the churchyard, then by the path between a fence and hedgerow beside the tennis courts. At the end of the path, walk by Tor Gardens and then take the first left. Beyond the houses the way bears left and the road reverts to a track and becomes wooded. Follow this track down towards the Lemon. Just before the bungalow at the foot look out for a Public Footpath sign on the right. Go through the gate here and follow the footpath. Where the path forks take the right hand way and walk beside the head of Puritans' Pit, a most impressive collapsed cavern in the limestone hillside, a good 50 feet in depth.

Once past the pit bear down left to meet the riverside path. The path here is not the easy, even way which it is on the north bank. Now it twists and turns with the meandering river and is badly eroded in parts where the river, regularly flooded from Dartmoor rains, undercuts the bank. However, follow the path downstream until you reach the pedestrian bridge which was passed near the beginning of the walk at the end of the meadow at **Bradley Manor**. Now retrace your steps beside the wall and mill leat and back through Baker's Park.

Newton Abbot is a town of some significance in South Devon. Famous neither for its beauty nor charm, it nevertheless commands a superb position at the confluence of several valleys and at the head of the Teign estuary. The town centre lies in a hollow between the Wolborough and Highweek Hills, each crowned by its parish church and each once the centre of a medieval settlement, respectively Newton Abbot and Newton Bushel. Many places were granted borough status in medieval times with the right to hold a weekly market and an annual fair; centres as small as Modbury, or even Denbury and Ermington were thus distinguished. The vast majority subsequently lost such status but Newton Abbot survived and indeed prospered. The weekly market includes a cattle market and attracts farmers and country folk from all across South Devon.

Bradley Manor dates from the thirteenth century when it was begun by the Bushels. It passed through the female line to the Yardes; Richard Yarde was appointed Sherriff of Devon in 1442-43. The Yardes remained lords of the manor until 1751, but at the beginning of the present century it was acquired by a descendant of the Yarde family, whose offspring still occupy the house. It is now owned by the National Trust so that there is an opportunity for the public to visit this delightful medieval manor house which nestles so peacefully amid the trees and meadow at the head of Bradley Woods.

West Ogwell manor house is a plain building which houses an Anglican sisterhood. The little church, of unknown dedication, is rather exceptional: a small cruciform building dating from *c*.1300. There are bare, whitewashed walls and high box pews, but no trace of the Victorian restorers. Concerned about the fate of this church when I lived in Newton Abbot I mentioned it in writing to the late Sir John Betjeman in 1978. His reply began 'West Ogwell Church is a winner', which was perhaps not his most poetic line. This 'delightful little church in a park' (*Guide to Parish Churches of England and Wales* , 1958) has since been declared redundant and is maintained under the Redundant Churches Fund.

WALK 2 BROADHEMPSTON

via Torbryan, Orley Common and Ambrook

Map: Torbay Sheet SX86/96

Map reference: 801663

Distance: 4½ miles (3½ miles by shorter route)

There are not very many rights of way in this part of South Devon which make sense in terms of a circular ramble of some substance. However, Broadhempston and Torbryan are both interesting and attractive villages and Orley Common is a fair-sized area of common land on a sloping limestone hillside which is a good place to go in search of wild flowers and butterflies.

The route of this ramble is in the shape of a figure eight so that it can be adapted in a number of ways. I will describe the two outer loops and finally the alternative inner route from Torbryan across fields to Broadhempston.

There are pubs at Broadhempston – the Monks Retreat and the Coppa Dolla Inn, and at Torbryan – the Church House Inn. There is also a general store in the former village. Orley Common provides an excellent site for a picnic.

From the little square in **Broadhempston**, with your back to the church and the pub, head down to the junction, at one corner of which stands the **post office/store**. Now leave the village by the upper lane. After about half a mile you reach **Waterford Cross**. Follow the lane on the far side, past **Coppa Dolla Farm**, over Collacombe Bridge which spans the Am Brook and on towards Tornewton.

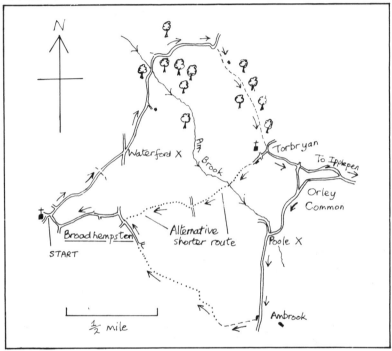

This way is by a quiet lane and the scenery is always pleasing, especially the latter half mile or so. Look out for the drive to **The Old Rectory**. Walk along here, past the impressive Victorian house and follow the track for a charming half mile towards Torbryan. You will most likely see a squirrel scurrying across your path to reach one or other of the copses which clothe the valley sides. You leave the path by an ornate iron gate to reach the lane. Turn right to reach **Torbryan**, a tiny village but one with an impressive church and attractive pub, both worthy of inspection.

Back at the junction turn right along the lane signposted to **Ipplepen**. After about a quarter of a mile, Orley Common can be reached from this lane – the main drive-in and parking place is further uphill towards Ipplepen.

From Orley Common bear left down the lane leading to **Poole** (for Broadhempston) and Ambrook. At **Poole Cross** turn left to reach **Ambrook**, the great house with its curious colonnaded west front can be seen across the valley. Just past the farmhouse on the right, about half a mile south of Poole Cross, take the track on the right. This is at first a sunken way with the main hedgebank on your left. Follow the hedge uphill; it eventually swings to the right. Follow the wire fence to reach a stile in the top left-hand corner. Cross a stone wall immediately on the left and head diagonally across the field towards a step stile. On the right about a mile distant you can see the church tower at Torbryan and, about a mile to its right, the church tower at Ipplepen. Cross the stile on the far side of the open field and follow the hedgebank on your right until you reach the works below. Turn right at the barn to reach the lane down into the village.

Alternative shorter route by field path from Torbryan to Broadhempston: Walk up past the **Church House Inn**, through a gate, and follow the stone wall on your left. As you crest the hill beside the barn you can see across the valley of the Am Brook and further on towards Broadhempston. Descend to the stile beside the gate and cross the boggy meadow in the valley bottom. The Am Brook is accompanied by a pair of channels running parallel with the main watercourse. This seems to provide a kind of primitive watermeadow. The sloping ground is full of water; if you stand on the limestone slab bridge across the main channel in the centre you can see water trickling down all along the banks. The spring growth here is certainly extremely lush.

Cross the stile on the far side and then head straight up the slope to reach the corner of the small hedged enclosure adjacent to the lane. At the time of writing there is an absence of stiles here; the right of way actually enters this enclosure at the projecting corner and reaches the lane at the five bar gate a few yards further on. Cross the lane and enter the field opposite by a gate. Follow the hedgerow on the left – on your right is the house called Simpson and straight ahead the buildings of Broadhempston. Climb the stile in the far corner of this field, crossing the bank beside the oak tree. The hedgerow brings you to a further stile, then an old stone slab stile drops you into the village. Bear right and left to reach the church.

Broadhempston is a scattered village which, approached from Tornewton, Torbryan or Ambrook, is dominated not by its church tower, as villages in South Devon most often are, but by a tall, dark blue grain silo. Its many old buildings are not always instantly recognisable under successive layers of cement rendering and whitewash, not to mention new doors and windows.

The Church of St Peter and St Paul is at the western extremity of the village, behind the Monks Retreat pub. At the entrance to the church are the remains of a medieval holy water stoop and, on the far side, the so called Devil's Doorway, a low opening built into the buttress between two windows. This is said to be where the evil spirit departed during baptism! Inside, the church is distinguished by twin arcades of white Beer stone with foliaged capitals, reminiscent of those at Torbryan. Also similar to Torbryan are the fifteenth century rood and parclose screens. Those at Broadhempston have restored upper sections; at Torbryan they were whitewashed by the then vicar to protect them from the depredations of the Puritans.

Both churches are worth visiting, Torbryan being a particular favourite of mine .... the plainness and grandeur of its whitewashed walls and arcades provides a striking contrast with its colourfully decorated screen and pulpit.

WALK 3   MARLDON

via Beacon Hill and Berry Pomeroy Castle

Map: Torbay Sheet SX 86/96

Map reference: 867636

Distance: 6 miles

This walk begins at St John's Church, in the old heart of the rather suburbanised village of Marldon, which is itself just outside the boundaries of Torbay Borough. The route follows a succession of field paths, tracks and lanes; one short stretch of road walking is unavoidable. Following this, the steep ascent of Beacon Hill may get you puffing but you will be rewarded with a spectacular panorama of Torbay near the summit. The valleys around Berry Pomeroy Castle are well wooded and the approach from the Castle Lodge may not be the most direct but it is the prettiest. The detour via Castle Mill affords a startling view of the ruins from the far side of the valley and the return from Afton Bridge to Marldon is by a succession of green lanes and field paths.

This is a good half day's ramble but could agreeably be adapted into a whole day's outing. Berry Pomeroy Castle with its surrounding woods is the half way stage and makes an excellent spot for a picnic. There is a good tea shop opposite the Castle entrance which is open daily from Easter until October. There is a pub, the Church House Inn, just below the church in Marldon.

From **Marldon Church**, climb the lane leading uphill to the left. Just past the former school buildings and directly opposite the church tower, bear left up some steps, through a gate and along a surfaced path, first rising and then following the contour across an open common with swings on the right. You reach a five-bar gate with an old iron kissing gate beside it. Go through here and follow the lane to the junction below which you bear right. Follow Marldon Hill Road past an old stone-built mounting block, the Primary School, Furzegood and bear right into **Westview Road.**

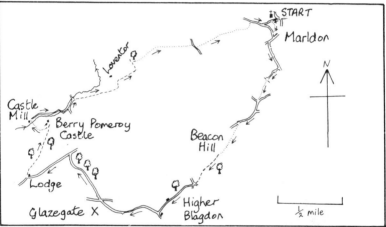

At the T-junction follow the footpath downhill between Numbers 20 and 21, then the road to the lane at the bottom. Head across the lane to reach the steps up to the stile opposite. Track across the field to the stile in the wire fence in the top left hand corner, then towards the five-bar gate ahead, and finally to the stile near the far corner of the last field. Here you drop down to **Farthing Lane** : bear left to reach the main road, where you turn right. There is no pavement here for a few yards until you reach the minor junction ahead. As you begin to ascend there is a pavement on the right; where this ends, cross the road and use the grass verge. Look out for a stile beside a gate set high in the bank on the left. The right of way is indicated by a Public Footpath sign on the opposite side of the road.

BETWIXT MOOR AND SEA

You climb directly up the slope here aiming for the pylon near the top of the hill. This is Beacon Hill, access to whose summit is restricted by a substantial stone wall just beyond the pylon. As the path begins to level out and you raise your eyes from the ground beneath you will enjoy an enormous view over the whole of Torbay and beyond.

Follow the beaten path beside the wall to an impressive ladder stile beside a five-bar gate in the corner of the field. Once over the stile you follow the hedged track downhill; a grove of pines lends a Mediterranean atmosphere. At the junction with four lanes you follow the second lane on the right which descends a steep-sided valley past **Higher Blagdon**. At the T-junction bear right, past the lane down to Torbay Aircraft Museum and on to **Glazegate Cross**. Cross the road and follow the lane opposite signposted to Berry Castle. The lane follows the contour: the valley on the right is too steep to be used for arable and is thickly wooded.

At the T-junction turn left to Berry Castle and leave the woods. This hedged lane soon leads you down to the **Castle Lodge** where you bear right across a stile beside the gate and follow the metalled track which gradually descends through woods in which beech trees and rhododendrons predominate. After about half a mile you suddenly emerge to be confronted by the twin massive entrance towers of the castle.

From **Berry Pomeroy Castle** the quickest return route is to remain on the southern side of the valley to reach Afton Bridge. However, at the café opposite the castle entrance one is invited to visit **Castle Mill**, and who could resist the grassy path which descends the primrosy banks down to the old mill nestling in the valley bottom? Once the mill is reached and Gatcombe Brook crossed, the lane on the far side provides a delightful walk along the valley.

Bear right and follow the lane beside woods on the left and the wet meadow with its marsh marigolds on the right. The view across to the ruined stone stacks of the castle provides an unexpected and completely different perspective.

Follow this lane (can you spot the old lime kiln?) to Afton Bridge and bear right along the track signposted to **Loventor Manor**. Just past the track leading to Chestnut Cottage you will find another marked with a Public Footpath sign; follow this past the few houses on the right between a pair of overgrown round stone pillars. The track descends to a bottom where, after rain, a stream flows. The track bears left and begins to ascend.

It is possible to follow this same track for half a mile or so to reach the lane opposite Aptor but there is an alternative and more direct right of way across fields. To follow the latter course bear right beside a low stone wall which surrounds a small copse just past the point where the track swings to the left. You may find this path overgrown but it is only a few steps to reach a gate into an open field. Follow the hedgerow on the right and enter the next field by a gate at the top. Head directly across the field towards a gate just to the left of a clump of trees. The right of way traverses the last field to reach the lane by a stile at a point about 25 yards to the left of the right hand corner. This stile is in the form of stone steps built into a wall. Once across here you bear right along the lane.

Almost immediately on your left, just to the right of the drive up to **Strainytor** look out for a Public Footpath sign indicating a steep and narrow path through the wood on the hillside. At the top of the wood you enter a field by a stile and follow the hedgerow on the left. Ahead you can see the bungalows of Marldon and to the right, across the valley, the bulk of Beacon Hill. The right of way is very clear and simply follows the hedgebank on the left; field crossings are facilitated by a number of good stiles. At the end of the fourth field you follow a passage between the hedgerow and a garden to reach the lane where you bear right towards Marldon. Along here you take a left fork down a 1:4 hill to reach the church.

Berry Pomeroy Castle: A well illustrated and inexpensive guide book may be purchased in the tea shop, so there is little purpose in providing but the briefest outline here. The castle is in an isolated spot and built on a spur of land which has a steep ascent on all sides save the approach from the Castle Lodge. It was the home of the Pomeroy family for five centuries following the Norman Conquest. In 1548 it was purchased by the Seymour family in whose ownership it remained until recently acquired by the Department of the Environment. The D of E have since been engaged in making safe the ruined façade of the once splendid mansion, begun but never completed by Sir Edward Seymour in the late sixteenth/early seventeenth centuries and which stands within the castle walls.

An interesting half hour or so may be spent inspecting the ruins and identifying the many features described in the official guide.

Berry Pomeroy Castle was often visited by early tourists to the West of England, enthusiastic as they were about ruins. W.G.Maton describes it thus in 1794:

> Berry Pomeroy is not more than a mile from Totnes. The great gate (with the walls of the south front), the apartments on the west side, and a turret or two, are the principal remains of the building, and they are so finely overhung with the branches of trees and shrubs that grow close to the walls, so beautifully matted with ivy, and so richly incrusted with moss, that they constitute the most picturesque objects that can be imagined. And when the surrounding scenery is taken into account,- the noble mass of wood fronting the gate, the bold ridges rising in the horizon, and the fertile valley opening to the east,- the ruins of Berry Pomeroy Castle must be considered as almost unparallelled in their effect.

WALK 4   TOTNES

via Ashprington and the River Dart

Map: South Devon Outdoor Leisure 20

Map Reference: 806603

Distance: 5½ miles

The route of this walk describes a figure of eight, albeit not a
nicely rounded such figure but rather one with all the appearance of the last strand of spaghetti on your plate – see the sketch
map. Nevertheless, the way reaches Ashprington via driveways
to Sharpham House and returns via lane, track and fieldpath to
cross the outward route at around the halfway stage.

This walk cannot be too strongly recommended. If you desire
a good half day's ramble on quiet byways with beautiful views
across the incomparable River Dart then this walk should not be
missed. The village of Ashprington is charmingly situated on a
declivity with the Church of St David at its head. The village
also possesses a pub – the Durant Arms, and a village store.
Opportunities for picnicking en route are also many.

Upon reaching Totnes you should make for **The Plains,** *i.e.*
the riverside on the west, or Totnes side, of the old town bridge.
From here you follow the river in a south-easterly direction, with
the former warehouses, now redeveloped, between the road and
the water. You progress past the beginnings of extensive timber

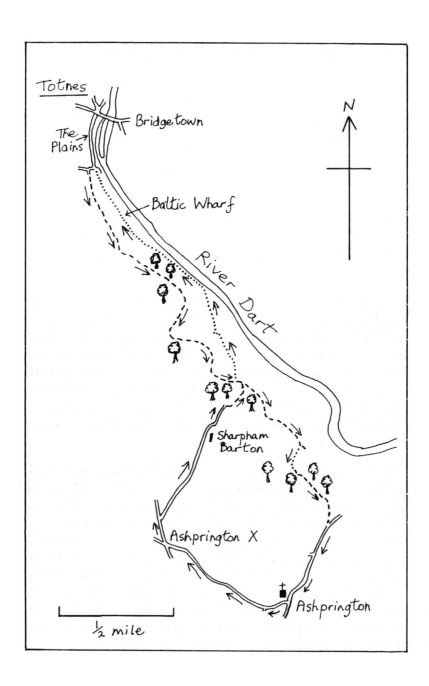

Totnes

Bridgetown

The Plains

Baltic Wharf

River Dart

N

Sharpham Barton

Ashprington X

Ashprington

½ mile

yards to reach the **Steam Packet Inn.** Bear right up the lane opposite the pub.

Notice a pair of well-preserved lime kilns at the side of the road immediately on the left. After a few yards you will find a track signposted Footpath to Ashprington. This is one of the approaches to Sharpham House which is situated about two miles to the south-east on a bluff overlooking the Dart. The drive is introduced by a set of four impressive granite gateposts.

Gaps in the hedgerow on the left reveal views over the timber yards at Baltic Wharf, the River Dart and Bridgetown beyond, its suburban aspect given perpective by the grey tower and nave of St John's Church, centrally located.

Simply follow the main track ahead. After crossing a stile beside a gate the way begins to descend slightly towards a narrow cleft in the hillside and the track becomes indistinct. Follow an even contour across the neck of the valley, keeping two oak trees just to your left until you reach a gate and stile on the opposite side. Now the track is unmistakable; another gate and stile is reached shortly, then the way follows a wire fence on your right. Hereabouts the vista opens out to give you extensive views over the widening river.

You cross another stile and gate and follow a clear track downhill beside a wood on your right .... then more stiles and a slight rise bring you to a pair of massive gateposts. Here you must look out for a wooden step stile on your right signposted Public Footpath: Ashprington. Cross the stile and climb the steep slope up the field to reach a stile about half way along the top edge. Enter the trees here and bear left along a shady woodland track which eventually finds a metalled lane; here bear right to reach **Ashprington** village. (On the left are gateposts marking the currently used approach to Sharpham House, two of which are topped with garlanded Grecian urns.)

To leave the village take the lane opposite the pub by the war memorial. Through gaps in the hedge along this lane you can look back in a south-easterly direction across the valley of Bow Creek towards the church and village of Cornworthy.

At **Ashprington Cross** bear right and soon bear right again – this way is signposted to **Sharpham Barton**. Where the descending track bifurcates take the left fork with a small barn on the left. Keep to the right to find a track between woods on your left and a hedge on your right. You emerge from the trees to reach the track you used on the first leg of the walk south. Cross the track and descend the hill directly to reach a five-bar gate opposite. Go through the gate and follow the beaten path through the young tree plantation, across the bottom of the following field and leave by a stile in the far corner. More stiles take you beside a barbed wire fence separating the firm ground underfoot from the reedy river bank to the right.

Emerge from the undergrowth to follow the bottom of an open field to a massive horizontal finger of Haytor granite which serves as stile in the field's far corner. You now descend to the water's edge which serves to give you a completely new relationship with the river. Seaweed is deposited at high water mark. Taste the water – yes, it is brackish. Ahead, beyond Baltic Wharf, rises the pinnacled tower of Totnes church.

Where the river bank becomes too obstructed with undergrowth and fallen trees look out for a path up through the hanging woods. You exit by a gate into an open field where you simply follow the beaten path to emerge at a point only a few yards below the signpost Public Footpath to Ashprington where you began.

Totnes is perhaps the most interesting, attractive and beautifully situated of all South Devon towns but this is not the place to discuss its charms. Alec Clifton-Taylor dealt lovingly with Totnes in his television series *Six English Towns* and a picture of its characteristic slate-hung buildings decorates the cover of the corresponding book.

The River Dart, too, has been eulogised, and not unfairly, by many writers, notably Ruth Manning-Sanders (*The River Dart*). The boat trip on the Dart from Totnes to Dartmouth is an experience not to be missed and is one which visitors to South Devon have been enjoying since tourism was invented. In 1854, one Walter White (*A Londoner's Walk to the Land's End*, 1855) describes his own trip as follows:

> At the landing-place, approached by a grove of chestnuts, lay the 'Undine', a pretty little steamer that plies to Dartmouth and back during the season, at hours dependent on the tide. We started at nine – a numerous company – and were presently in the centre of the channel shooting swiftly down the stream .... On speeds the vessel between rich meadows and teeming orchards, and hills cultivated to the summit, the dark red soil showing along the margin of the crops. Then higher hills hidden in glorious woods, here and there a red crag peeping through, and ivy and creepers so luxuriant you might fancy yourself among tropical vegetation.

The Dart, White concludes, is 'no unworthy rival to the Wye', the river so beloved of William Gilpin and seekers after 'the picturesque'.

Ruth Manning-Sanders described Ashprington as 'a very pretty and tidily arranged village' and this description seems as fitting today as in 1951. One oddity is the smooth, polished slate slabs used on the steps beside the church's lych gate. And does it not seem curious that a stone stile should have been provided right beside the lych gate? Perhaps the stile was there first.

WALK 5   HARBERTONFORD

via Rolster Bridge, East Leigh and Harberton

Map: South Devon Outdoor Leisure 20

Map reference: 783568

Distance: 5½ miles

This is a straightforward, undemanding walk through unspec-
tacular, though very pleasant, South Devon countryside. Harbertonford is situated on the busy A381 Totnes-Kingsbridge
road. Like most small villages, a public car park is not provided
and parking can be a problem. However, there is usually a space
to be found on the triangle in front of the church. The route
follows a mixture of field paths, unmade tracks and quiet
country lanes. The sister village of Harberton is reached after
about two thirds of the course has been completed. This is
an attractive village with a fine church, splendid pub and
interesting mix of domestic buildings.

From **Harbertonford** take the lane which leaves the main road
to the left of the church. Once past **Old Mill** the buildings cease
and the lane follows the valley of the River Harborne, glimpses
of which can be seen through gaps in the hedgerow on the left.

After almost a mile the lane is signposted right to **The Old
Mill**; here you bear down left to cross the old stone bridge
indicated as Rolster Bridge on the Outdoor Leisure map. You
rise on the far side between farm buildings to reach a gate just

past the bungalow on the right. A Public Footpath sign indicates a right of way across the field. Head directly across this rather elongated field, up valley, on an even contour, for about 500 yards, towards the hedgerow at the far end. The hedge makes a dog-leg bend – head for a stile in its furthermost crook.

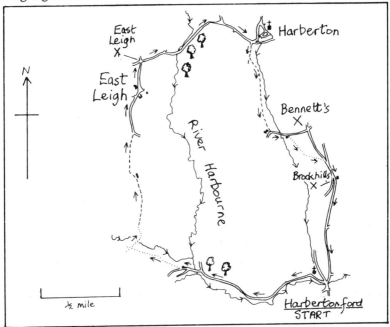

Once in the next field the right of way continues further up the valley but intersects a second right of way near the far left corner. Now change direction by following this second right of way northwards. Bear right to cross the brook in the bottom left corner of this small field. The bridge is made up of slate slabs and old wooden railway sleepers.

Follow the hedgebank on the left uphill through two fields via two broken gates until you emerge onto a good clear track between hedgebanks. This takes you past a dilapidated barn and after about half a mile reaches a gate just before the lane. Continue in the same northerly direction to **East Leigh.**

The Pathfinder map indicates a short cut across fields at this point. The track on the right to Friendsleigh takes you to the beginning of a path between walls, but the way is completely blocked by rubbish and undergrowth. This short-cut would take you to the valley bottom and would reduce two sides of a triangle to a straight line but, at the time of writing, I must report that this way is impractical.

Continue through East Leigh to **Eastleigh Cross** and bear right. Notice the Victorian post box in the stone wall of a house on your right. At the valley bottom stands a cottage dated 1893 just to the right of which the unusable field path from East Leigh emerges. Climb up, past a wooded slope on your right. As you crest the hill you can see ahead to the tower of **Harberton Church.**

After exploring the village, backtrack to the lane by which you entered the village. There is a wide opening reserved for turning buses – this marks the start of a pleasant track which leads south towards Key's Englebourne. After about 100 yards the track forks left – take this apparently lesser way to follow the valley until you emerge onto a lane. Bear left to the valley bottom and the house called **Wyses Englebourne.**

Once again you are faced with the possibility of cutting a corner by taking field paths but again this is not as easy as it could be. The way is by a gate immediately past the house. Climb up the slope and head diagonally across this field to a gate in the top left corner. Cross the next field to the far left corner. Patient prodding will reveal evidence of a gap in the stone wall which the overgrown hedge has obscured. I found it necessary to reach the lane by the entrance gates to Great Englebourne a few yards further on. It must be stressed that this is not a right of way so, in the absence of a practical crossing to reach the road, you may feel it wise to follow the lane up from Wyses Englebourne and to bear right at Bennet's Cross.

You have now reached the main road which you must follow south, but mercifully only for a few yards, to reach the last stage of the walk. Take the left fork at **Brockhills Cross** and follow the Old Road down to Harbertonford.

Harberton is a substantial village, its buildings attractively arranged on a sloping site. St Andrew's Church dominates the scene with its high, buttressed tower complete with stair turret. Its large, Perpendicular windows shed much light on the riches of its interior. The exquisitely detailed and brightly painted rood screen will immediately attract the visitor; angelic figures in the panels date from the Victorian Restoration which, according to Baring-Gould (*Devon*, 1907), were painted by an amateur, being portraits of the young ladies of the congregation. The original medieval panels can be seen in glass cases at the far side of the nave.

After the screen you will admire the finely carved stone pulpit. And don't miss the comparatively restrained but dignified Norman font of red sandstone near the door.

The Church House Inn close by the pub claims to be thirteenth century though Hoskins says sixteenth. He also notes that East Leigh, among others in the parish, was a Domesday manor.

Harbertonford came after Harberton, when a bridge was built to span the River Harborne some three or four centuries ago. It was made a separate parish in 1860 when St Peter's was erected. Harbertonford was busy with industry possessing, as it did until recent years, a woollen mill and an edge tool mill.

WALK 6   CORNWORTHY

via Tuckenhay and Bow Creek

Map: South Devon Outdoor Leisure 20

Map Reference: 829555

Distance: 3 miles

This comparatively short walk offers an exceptional variety of
scenery and points of interest. The village of Cornworthy is of a
similar size and has a similar aspect to Ashprington which is
about a mile away, as the crow flies, on the far side of Bow
Creek. Both communities are strung out on a hillside below their
respective churches. Yet Cornworthy seems to belong more to
the countryside – agricultural vehicles trundling up and down its
main street are not an uncommon sight.

From the village the route follows the road out in a westerly
direction to Abbey Cross and the fascinating remains of an old
priory. A little further on a change of direction takes you along a
green lane to the surprising community of Tuckenhay. No
village clustering beneath its church tower here – in fact, no
church at all – but extensive former mills which reveal Tuckenhay's past as a thriving centre of rural industry.

In the valley bottom you enjoy another change of scene: a
stroll beside the banks of the tidal Bow Creek – several miles
from the open sea, but possessing many of the natural features of

the Dart Estuary itself. The Bow Creek is left by a track which leads you back to Cornworthy Church.

From **Cornworthy Church** you head due west by taking the road down the hillside through the village. At **Abbey Cross** you should not miss the remains of the former priory.

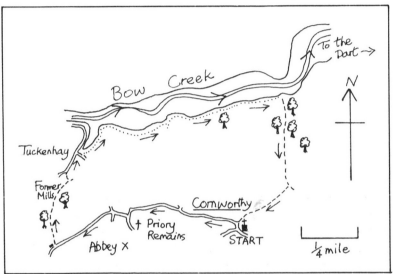

From the ruin you continue on the lane towards Tuckenhay; this leads you down the slope of Corkscrew Hill. Across the field to your right you will see the top of a chimney belonging to the mill buildings at Tuckenhay. As you near the bottom of the hill look out for a triangular road warning sign. Just below the sign and above a small barn tucked into the corner of the next field is an unmade track between hedgebanks. Follow this way between fields and through woods above the valley of the River Wash. The path soon emerges just above the ornate and carefully restored clock tower of the impressive old mill building in **Tuckenhay**. As you approach the building you will see what appears to be a leat with a sluice gate still intact. A tablet in the wall reads, 'H.S. 1889'.

47

Follow the metalled lane down towards a crossing of the River Wash which is a rapidly flowing stream. Bear right to follow the road down towards Bow Creek. Cross the stone bridge on the right. About 25 yards from the bridge, just past **Brook House** , there are, on the left, two steps up to a stile signposted Public Footpath. A few yards further on cross a wooden step stile. Follow a narrow way between a fenced field on the right and the estuary on the left. Climb a stile and follow the edge of the field to the right.

Keep on a fairly even contour just above the tree-lined shore. Eventually the line of trees drops down to a gate in the far corner of the field. The right of way is marked by a yellow arrow. Go through the gate and follow the beaten path until you reach the shore. After about half a mile heading downstream you reach a five-bar gate where a yellow arrow pointing rightwards marks a change of course.

It is well worth looking beyond the gate towards a couple of well-preserved lime kilns built into the bank on the right and, further on still, to the ruined hulks of two old craft lying, half-submerged, in the estuarine mud. Looking beyond Bow Creek you can see across the River Dart to Duncannon.

Follow the hedgerow on the left until you reach a point where the field narrows and you find yourself following a track. At the cross track bear right and follow the gentle ascent back to **Cornworthy** church, via a farmyard.

Cornworthy Church is dedicated to St Peter. The main fabric of the building is fourteenth/fifteenth century, although there is a Norman font. The largely granite arcades lead the eye to a medieval screen, though somewhat restored. Through the screen on the right is an impressive looking monument dated 1610. But the most striking feature of the church is its Georgian character. This is revealed in its box pews, brass candelabrum, windows of clear glass and a dominating pulpit overhung by a magnificent sounding board. This refitting was carried out in 1788, during the record-breaking incumbency of the Rev. Charles Barter who was vicar here for 71 years!

The intriguing remains at Abbey Cross are of those of an Augustinian nunnery founded in the early thirteenth century, only to be abandoned following the dissolution of the monasteries in 1536 under Henry VIII. The gatehouse remains: the larger archway is slightly pointed and formerly accepted wheeled traffic and those on horseback whilst the smaller round-arched doorway to the left was for those on foot. The structure is built of ashlar stone blocks with granite employed for the piers, arches and vaulting. A doorway inside the main gate leads to a circular stone staircase which turns through 540 degrees and emerges above the arch.

Tuckenhay is situated in the valley of the River Wash and the shores of Bow Creek. The diminutive but spirited Wash once provided water power for a corn mill and two paper mills, one of which survived until the 1960s. The old mill building is now redeveloped as holiday flats. There are warehouses and quays lower down beside Bow Creek. Local basalt was once exported from here to serve as roadstone in the streets of London. Another interesting reminder of an industrial past is a gas house dated 1806.

WALK 7   DITTISHAM

via Bosomzeal, Downton and Old Mill Creek

Map: South Devon Outdoor Leisure 20

Map Reference: 865551

Distance: 5 miles

This ramble takes in the hills and combes to the south and west of the former port and present ferry crossing point of Dittisham, on the banks of the Dart. An initial mile of (mostly) gentle climbing raises you from near sea level to the summit of Fire Beacon Hill, at around 530 feet. After descending the hillside through about 150 feet the route begins to rise again via Lapthorn and Downton Farm to reach the main road at Downton Cross, at 548 feet. A lane is followed to Kingston and then field paths to reach a bridge across the combe at an indicated 117 feet. From here a small climb to around 250 feet gives you some wonderful views across the Dart before returning to Dittisham.

On entering **Dittisham** follow the **P** signs down along **Riverside Road** to reach the car park and toilets on the edge of a field facing the Dart. From here you follow the indicated path beside the swings to Lower Dittisham and Quay. In the corner of the field you bear right up the enclosed path to **Lower Dittisham**. Follow the path via a wooden kissing gate and up some steps to reach a stone slab stile which drops you onto the lane; here turn left and head through the village.

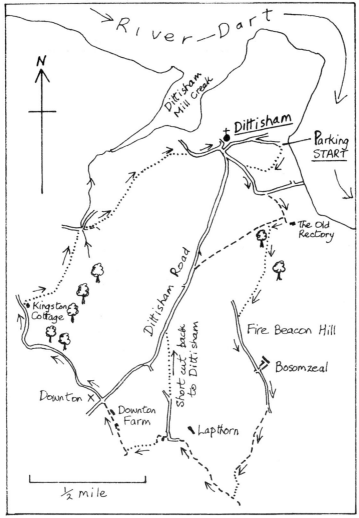

At the fork ahead do not bear left but take the right turning named **The Level** and indicated as Footpath to Dartmouth. As you approach **The Old Rectory** you can see through the trees to the left across the great wide sweep of the Dart above Greenway Quay, and closer at hand the far narrower crossing between that point and Dittisham. Just before the entrance gates to the Rectory look out for a dilapidated sign Footpath to Dartmouth pointing to the right across a triangle at this junction. Follow this wide track uphill until you reach a gate on the left.

Cross the stile beside the gate and follow the open track up and around the hillside. As height is gained you can look back down onto the rectory and take in a long view up the Dart. Cross the stile beside the gate ahead and carry on with the hedgebank on the right to cross the next stile not far on. Cross the field to a point just to the left of a projecting hedgerow and then straight on to leave the field by a stile in the far corner. Bear left at the lane.

You very soon reach the crest of this hill, interestingly indicated on the Outdoor Leisure map as Fire Beacon Hill. Presumably this high point served as a place for raising fires to serve as guides or warnings to shipping entering the Dart Estuary; a fire was lit to warn of the approaching Armada four centuries ago.

Now you begin to descend: **Bosomzeal** is a range of buildings whose handsomeness certainly lives up to that of its name. This settlement is situated at the top of a combe leading down to Old Mill Creek and, although we are within easy range of the hilltop suburbs of Dartmouth this is a very quiet and peaceful spot. At 10.30 one dull, cold March morning as I was walking here an owl flew over my head and landed on the overhanging hedge to get a good look at this strange human shape. I managed to get quite close before he flapped off.

Look out for a gate on the right indicating Public Footpath. Enter the field and follow the open track. The view now reveals itself – to the south-east you can see the confluence of Old Mill Creek with the Dart; in the distance the mouth of the Dart and the open sea beyond; on the intervening hill stands Dartmouth Naval College. Beyond the next gate the footpath follows a hedge on the left. Leaving the field at the next gate you make a half right by heading down the track; fork left at the bottom by going through the gate and following the stony path downhill.

When the stream at the bottom is reached you go through a gate to reach a track crossing from right to left. Bear right and back up the hill towards the scattered buildings at **Lapthorn**. At the end of the path bear left along a metalled lane. If you follow the metalled lane as it swings uphill to the right you will eventually meet the Dittisham road and this provides a short cut back to the village.

The route suggested here leaves the metalled lane at the point where it bears away right; instead, make your way along the hedged track to the right of the barn. Bear left before the gate ahead and then through the next gate where you will spot a Public Footpath sign in the bank on the right. Scramble up the bank here and follow the hedgerow on the right to reach the gate in the far corner. Turn right along the wide track, past **Downton Farm** to reach the main road.

After taking in the wide view at **Downton Cross** continue by the lane directly opposite. Carry on until you reach **Kingston Cottage** where you will find a Public Footpath sign just below the house. This indicates the right of way through the drive of the house. At the bottom bear left up the slope and right to enter a field by a stile. Walk on with the hedgebank on your left. Cross one stile and then straight on until the hedgerow takes a dog-leg bend to the left; from this point track across and down the hillside to reach a stile at a point about 20 yards to the left of the valley bottom.

Bear right on the lane, cross the stream (notice the old, narrow bridge on the left beside the more recent crossing). Do not ascend the stony track opposite but go through the gate on the right of the lane – as you approach it you will find, amid the ivy, a signposted stile on its right. Follow the beaten way past the small clump of trees; once past here cross the bottom of the field above a drainage pipe and head up the slope beside a hedgerow on your right.

On the brow of the hill you look down onto Dittisham Mill Creek, comprising one or two cottages, a few boats and what looks like an old lime kiln. Cross the next stile and follow the hedge. At the last stile it is worth looking back up river – the village of Stoke Gabriel is easily seen on the opposite bank. Now **Dittisham** lies before you, the church tower straight ahead.

Dittisham, with its plum orchards, is a village beloved of the old guide books, and justifiably so. At high tide the great sweep of the river over to Galmpton Creek and the tree-clad slopes on the far banks lend the prospect all the appearance of a great lake. The birthplace of the Gilbert family, of whom Sir Humphrey Gilbert is the most famous (he it was who, in 1573, laid claim to Newfoundland) is at Greenway on the wooded hill directly opposite. The house seen today was formerly the home of Agatha Christie.

Dittisham includes Higher Dittisham, which lies about the crossroads above the church. St George's Church is entered by an unusual turnstile type of gate. The church is built mainly of slate but with quite a lot of red sandstone blocks; the interior has Beer stone arcades. Notable features include the 'wine glass' pulpit, also termed, perhaps more aptly, 'chalice shaped'. This elegant structure is carved in stone, not wood, and exhibits painted panels of an early date. The ancient red sandstone font is massively proportioned.

A lane leads past the Red Lion pub towards Lower Dittisham and eventually bears left to reach the Ferry Boat Inn. A stroll down river along the shore reveals the maritime face of the village.

WALK 8   DIPTFORD

via the River Avon, Bickham Bridge and Gara Bridge

Map: South Devon Outdoor Leisure 20

Map Reference: 728568

Distance: 6½ miles (or 5½ to return via Bickham Bridge)

This is an undemanding but extremely pleasant walk which follows the River Avon downstream on its eastern bank and back upstream on its western. This stretch of the Avon valley is very quiet and unspoilt, without a public highway for most of its length but only the occasional settlement and remains of the former branch railway line to Kingsbridge.

From whichever direction you enter the village you will reach the crossroads at its centre; from there head down towards the church. The road outside the church is wide enough to allow parking for a few cars and you are unlikely to be causing anyone inconvenience by leaving your car in this cul-de-sac. The old Church House stands opposite the church gate but, unlike so many church houses in Devon villages betwixt moor and sea, this one is not a public house but a private one. Nor is there a pub or any other place of refreshment on or near the route so, if you wish to devote more than half a day to complete this ramble, you will have to take your own victuals with you. There are certainly many excellent spots at which to picnic.

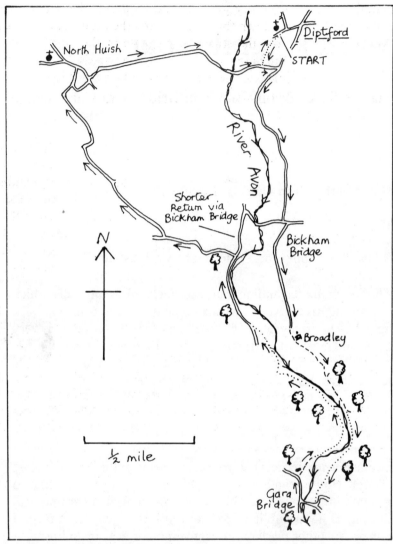

At the end of the cul-de-sac flanked by **Diptford church** and **Church House** you will find a step stile leading into a field. The prospect which this affords, of field and hillside, is gained within seconds of locking your car door and could not be more welcome. Following the direction of the Public Footpath sign at the stile you head down the field towards the group of buildings on the right. Cross the stile beside a gate in the bottom right hand corner. From here you can see ahead towards the steep and wooded slopes, indeed, the almost gorge-like proportions, of the Avon valley. You soon cross another step stile and then an old stone slab stile to reach the lane.

It is necessary to make a short dog-leg detour by bearing left up the lane and then sharp right at the T-junction ahead; now follow this lane south to Bickham Bridge. At first the way climbs to reach the brow of a hill. Here there are views over the valley close at hand and back towards Diptford, well marked from this angle by its church spire, and much further beyond towards the heights of Dartmoor. The lane loses altitude but continues to run parallel with the Avon but at a level of 50 feet or so above the riverside meadows.

As you emerge at the cottages you bear left and then sharp right. Bickham Bridge crosses the river on the right; the lane you are now following is signposted to **Broadley**. As you approach this valley farm the lane begins to descend more rapidly and the view opens out across the valley towards the wooded slopes on the opposite bank. Immediately below can be seen the slightly embanked course of the old railway crossing the meadow.

Broadley comprises an interesting group of buildings. Be sure not to miss the old store on staddle stones which perches on a small bluff just before the main group is reached; the latter are attractively ranged around a courtyard. The old stone walls are worthy of inspection: the main constituent is the local slaty rock but there are also large lumps of white milkstone, also found locally, and small boulders of granite – sometimes fine grained and pinkish, sometimes the greyer and course-grained granite like that of Haytor – but all pieces which are smooth and well rounded, suggesting that they have been taken from the bed of the Avon, having been brought down from the moor by the river.

Once past these buildings the metalled lane reverts into a stony track as it enters woodland. Several small streams run down the hillside to cross the way and flow into the Avon. At a low point, on a level with the river, one of these streams flows under the railway track by a small bridge through which the river can be seen. Just after this little bridge the main track bears uphill and slightly to the left. Here you must take the right fork and descend a little to follow the right of way beside the river.

Very soon the low embankment of the old railway heads for the river bank: this marks a point where the track switched banks. If you scramble to the river shore you can see the remains of the piers on either bank and, if the river is low, of the central pier. The broken masonry comprises blocks of Devonian limestone, pale grey and veined with calcite. If not in flood, the river here is surprisingly wide, shallow, clear and fast flowing.

The path now climbs up through woodland above a fairly precipitous slope down to the river. You can see a weir below and a leat which I guess once drove a wheel in a mill at Gara Bridge (the old O.S. maps indicate a corn mill), though it now supplies fresh water to ponds in a trout farm a little downstream. This lovely woodland path, clothed with ferns and moss, leads down to the small community at **Gara Bridge**. This marks the half way stage of the ramble and the point at which the river is crossed. Bear right to cross the old railway track – notice the well preserved and now extended buildings of the former Gara Bridge Railway Station on the left – and the river.

Bear right at the T-junction and follow the lane north. As the road swings away to the left look out for the Public Footpath sign on the right. Head right in the indicated direction, past the three cottages on the left to cross the stile ahead; the river is below a few yards to the right. Follow thr right of way across an open meadow, then through woodland (indicated on the Pathfinder map as Garaland Copse). Near the end of this wood the main track bears left uphill – at this point look out for a stile just ahead.

Cross the field by descending to the stream at its centre – here you can see many fragments of milkstone – and up the far side. A yellow arrow on a telegraph pole here confirms that you are on the right course. Soon you cross a stile to follow the path. Here slate is exposed where the path cuts into the slope. There is a beautiful prospect upstream; it seems a pity to have to leave the river at this point but the right of way, marked by a yellow arrow, leads through the woods towards a stile.

The path, climbing gently, soon reaches the lane: bear right, and happily the lane follows the river once again. When the junction beside the railway bridge is reached you are presented with a choice of routes back to Diptford. You can either cross the railway track to reach Bickham Bridge and then bear left to retrace your steps, or continue by the lane you have been following, past **Bickham** and **Southern House**, to reach the tiny village of **North Huish**. The latter is a good way to approach the church of St Mary which has a spire and a noble outline, even if it is slightly disappointing on closer inspection.

After reaching the church you must retrace your steps until you find the lane bearing left along a mainly straight stretch downhill to cross the river below Diptford. The railway once crossed the road by a bridge, the piers of which remain beside the road. Here most of the masonry appears to be composed of greenstone. Cross the river bridge and follow the lane until you reach the old stone slab stile which leads to the way across the fields and back to Diptford church.

BETWIXT MOOR AND SEA

The **Kingsbridge Branch Railway** left the GWR main line at South Brent and headed almost due south to reach Kingsbridge, 'the capital of the South Hams', in a little over 12 miles. There were stations at Avonwick, Gara Bridge, and Loddiswell with the terminus at Kingsbridge. For most of its length the line follows the valley of the River Avon and constantly switches from one bank to the other. This fact accounts for many of its 48 bridges; where the line leaves the valley south of Loddiswell it goes underground via Sorley Tunnel.

The main line to Plymouth opened in 1848, and in the same year a coach service from Kinsgbridge began but it was another 45 years before the town had its own rail link. There were ambitious plans to drive the line on to Salcombe and to extend the Dart Valley line from Totnes to Dartmouth, around the coast to Torcross and thence to Kingsbridge. From Kingsbridge a line was planned to progress westwards via Modbury to Yealmpton. However, the motor age was dawning,, and in 1909 the GWR began motor bus services and these rapidly developed to link up even the smallest South Hams communities. Had these additional railway lines been built, Kingsbridge would have been a local railway junction; in the event it served as a junction for many of the bus routes. In addition, GWR took over the Kingsbridge-Salcombe steamer service in 1929.

Single unit diesel railcars were introduced on the line in 1961 but such modernisation was short lived. Passenger and freight traffic declined steadily in the late 1950s and the Beeching axe was inevitable: the last train ran in September 1963 and thus ended the 69 year life span of the Kingsbridge branch. Its popular name was the Primrose Line, so commonplace was that wild flower on the bosky banks of the Avon valley. The line was almost, but not quite, bought and saved by a local preservation movement. Opportunities for walking the line today are, unfortunately, very limited – it would undoubtedly make a splendid right of way from end to end.

WALK 9   LODDISWELL

via the River Avon, Old Railway Track and Newmill Bridge

Map: South Devon Outdoor Leisure 20

Map Reference: 719486

Distance: 4 miles

The hill top village of Loddiswell may by unlovely but the valley landscape so near at hand is indeed beautiful and this is a most enjoyable and interesting walk. There are no steep inclines save the final haul up from Newmill Bridge, though this is not too taxing.

A track beside Loddiswell church leads down to the Avon and a riverside path is followed upstream to reach an old railway bridge. On the opposite bank the walker has a choice between a permissive path along the old railway track or a woodland path which runs beside it. Both ways eventually reach a lane at the former Loddiswell Station. The river is followed downstream to Newmill Bridge.

Loddiswell has two pubs and several shops.

From whichever direction **Loddiswell** is approached, signs will direct you to the public car park. From here you weave your way between the buildings and head towards the **church**. Make for the track just to the left of the tower; at the T-junction ahead bear left and then sharp right. At a little of junction of ways

61

ahead carry on past **Ham Butts** and down towards **Reads Farm**.
As the track begins to descend you can see across the steep
wooded valley of the Avon towards Woodleigh church atop the
hill opposite.

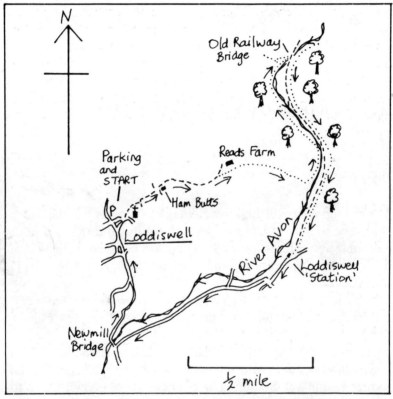

The track dips more steeply as the farm is approached; look
out for a green steel gate on the right just before reaching the
farm buildings. At this point a Public Footpath sign indicates
the right of way along the track to the right of the buildings and
further on, following now one side, now the other, a little stream
flowing down this cleft in the hillside towards the Avon. Along
here you will see the first of many yellow arrows indicating the
right of way.

As you near the river you will see a pair of Public Footpath signs in the bottom corner. Bear left and follow the river upstream for about half a mile. The way is rough in parts but well endowed with stiles and yellow arrows. The prospect in this steep-sided valley is quite enthralling; in spring the ground is covered with bluebells. There is much fallen timber, sometimes blocking the path. The fallen wood provides an anchor for pennywort, in addition to the more usual moss and ferns. The river itself is always close at hand, at first narrow and deep and swiftly moving, then wide and sluggish above a weir. A leat, now dried up, starts just above this weir, the path following it for some distance. At one point the path crosses the leat by way of an old sluice gate.

A little beyond the weir you reach the edge of the woods and enter a meadow but still follow the way beside the river. As you reach a little brook flowing into the river, a yellow arrow and Public Footpath sign indicate a way to the left. Ignore this but continue in the same direction towards the old **railway bridge**. This splendid piece of railway architecture is worth a second glance. The main structure is built of roughly squared blocks of slate, the coping stones are granite and the bridge, which crosses the river at an acute angle, possesses arches in which the several thicknesses of brick spanning the arches gradually change their angle of repose from one side to the other – the skill and dexterity of the bricklayers employed here has to be admired.

Scramble up the embankment to reach the bridge and cross the river. Notices among the trees on your left inform you that the woods here belong to the Woodland Trust. The right of way is by a path which is clearly discernible at the foot of the slope and runs parallel to the left of the old railway track. You may wish to follow the old track for a while to absorb something of the atmosphere of the former Kingsbridge branch line, once aptly known as The Bluebell Line. After about a hundred yards you will hear once again the rush of water as the track runs beside the Avon.

If you wish, you can climb across to reach the right of way beside the track. This is a well maintained path which is provided with duckboards at points where boggy ground is traversed and where you are likely to see marsh marigold. The end of the path also marks the end of the railway track. Here is a stile and a notice indicating that the track is a permitted path, that is to say not a right of way but a privately owned path to which the public is normally permitted access.

Carry on until you reach the road. The house on the right is the former Loddiswell Station – necessarily situated in the valley and some distance from the hill-top village of Loddiswell. The chimney stacks and window surrounds bear an unmistakable resemblance to those at the old Gara Bridge Station seen on the walk from Diptford. Notice the Victorian letterbox embedded in the rock face opposite; the last time I passed it the mouth was loosely sealed by a piece of sponge bearing the legend 'To stop snails'.

Follow the lane under the railway bridge (at this point much wider than single track). Very soon you will spot a crossing point over a stone wall leading into the field beside the river. An old boundary marker inscribed 'Great Western Railway Companies Boundary 1896' here serves as a step. Follow the riverside path downstream. As you approach the bridge you will see an old mill on your right, now known as **Avon Mill, Garden Centre and Nursery**; most likely this mill was the object of the leat which left the river back upstream below the railway bridge.

Cross the stile at the bridge and bear left and then right along the lane. Follow the river downstream until **Newmill Bridge** is reached. Cross the river here and pass by the attractive group of buildings to the left. Traces of a dried up leat can be seen to the right: presumably once the source of power at New Mill. The track begins to rise, at first gently, then more steeply, to give one final view over the beautiful but secluded valley of the Avon before re-entering Loddiswell.

Loddiswell is not the most attractive village betwixt moor and sea: even Hoskins describes it as 'large, untidy and planless'. You feel that the open space in front of the church could be a real asset to a village the size of Loddiswell but it does seem to be rather wasted. One of the ugliest buildings here is an angular, derelict looking structure *c.* 1960, which upon enquiry I found to be a former egg packing station that has been awaiting change of use or redevelopment for the previous few years.

From this 'village square' the church seems to be standing apart, somewhat forlornly, the tower and nave of the old building shielding the eyes of those lying in the graveyard behind from the depredations of the present. The church is further cut off by being kept locked, at least so I have found it to be. A set of stocks in the porch seems to threaten the intending visitor. One handsome and indeed striking building is the great Congregational church which is situated in a commanding position at the centre of the village; nearby is its own graveyard.

White's Devon Directory of 1878 notes that Loddiswell Congregational Church was erected in 1864 at a cost of £1,000, and describes it as 'a substantial and commodious building', and that half of it was paid for by one Richard Peek. My enquiries at the West Country Studies Library in Exeter led me to a *History of Loddiswell* produced by the village primary school. According to this publication, Richard Peek was born in Loddiswell in 1782. In 1807 he walked to London to seek his fortune. As he was crossing London Bridge he met a Quaker whom he knew and this good fellow found the young Peek a position with Sanderson and Barclays, tea merchants. Having learnt his trade, Richard and his brother William set up on their own and eventually became the largest tea merchants in London. Richard Peek crowned his success by being chosen as High Sheriff for London and Middlesex. He returned to live at Hazlewood just outside the village; Loddiswell Chapel is one of several endowed by the Peeks, and they paid entirely for Loddiswell School, now the village primary school.

WALK 10   WEST CHARLETON

via Frogmore and Frogmore Creek

Map: South Devon Outdoor Leisure 20

Map Reference: 753426

Distance: 4½ miles

This exhilarating ramble follows one of the few rights of way alongside the Kingsbridge Estuary, albeit by one of its branches, Frogmore Creek. The village of West Charleton and the hamlet of Frogmore are both situated on the road which runs from Start Bay to Kingsbridge.

Field paths lead north from West Charleton up a valley to reach an old green lane which climbs to around 300 feet and affords tremendous views. From Frogmore a footpath leads for over a mile beside the creek almost as far as the old slate quarries for which Charleton was once famous. After leaving the shore the way crosses fields back to West Charleton. Parking is pretty well impossible in Frogmore, and for that reason the recommended starting point is West Charleton. Both communities possess a pub, the the Globe Inn at Frogmore having a strong nautical flavour – even the walls are papered with navigation maps. This is a varied walk and the waterside section certainly adds to its attraction. For this reason it is advisable to walk along the creek when the tide is up,- unless, of course, your main passion is birdlife, when you might prefer to walk here when the tide is ebbing. Before the path turns inland it reaches the beach opposite Ham Point and this is an excellent place to enjoy a picnic.

West Charleton's pub is the Ashburton Arms. The car park here is strictly for pub patrons but the street beside the pub, Charleton Way, leads to a housing estate where there is ample room for a visitor to park without causing residents any obstruction.

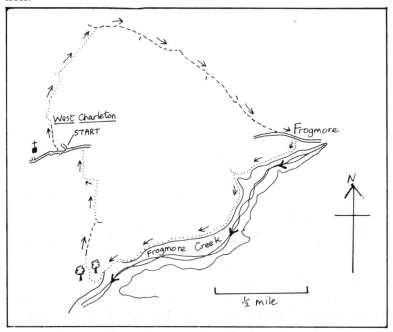

Facing the main road at the entrance to **Charleton Way** bear right, in the direction of Kingsbridge. Very soon you reach a grassy entrance to a path marked by a pair of white poles. Follow the path above some houses, pass a yellow arrow, then another, and arrive at a stile at the end of a hedge. Cross here and head through the field beside a stream to the far left corner. Carry on slightly uphill to a gate and a Public Footpath sign. Follow the beaten path along the hillside a little above the stream to reach a stone wall with projecting steps. Climb these and make your way down to cross the stream at a junction of ways marked by a pair of footpath signs.

Upright slate slabs are here used as an unusual and interesting means of shoring up the hedgebank at the top of the field. About 20 yards upstream from this crossing are a pair of yellow arrows on a telegraph pole pointing in either direction. Continue to track the stream up the little valley past a patch of furze and through an iron gate. Leave this last open field by climbing the stone steps set in the wall.

Once in the green lane bear right and climb steadily through about 150 feet over the next quarter mile. This lane is of considerable proportions. Could it once have been the main road from Frogmore to Dodbrooke/Kingsbridge – perhaps before the bridge across the mouth of Bowcombe Creek was constructed?

Over the brow of the hill a crossroads is reached. The gate on the right provides a good place to take in the view down Frogmore Creek to the Kingsbridge Estuary and beyond to the hills on the far shore. Another place to stand and stare is reached at the T-junction a little further beyond. Bear right here and continue to descend until you join the main road on the edge of **Frogmore**. The local pub, the Globe Inn, is straight down the road.

The next stage of the ramble is midway between the point at which you join the road and the Globe. Look out for a Public Footpath sign between cottages on the opposite side of the road. Go through the gate ahead and enter the field overlooking Frogmore Creek. Head across the field towards the stone step stile in the far right corner. The footpath now tracks along the edges of succeeding fields just above the shore. There are numerous field crossings but all are pretty clear and easy so there is no need to describe the route in detail.

About a hundred yards below a dilapidated and rather gaunt looking barn you bear left across a stream and through a hedge. Track across a rather scrubby piece of ground to a corner (where there is a Public Footpath sign pointing inland) and beyond to follow this small inlet back to the creek. Simply follow the path on the field edges above the creek. Eventually a yellow arrow will direct you down onto the beach. It certainly is good to arrive at this point at around high tide.

Follow the beach to the wood ahead and head up the signposted track which leads straight up through the trees. Pass through a gate to reach a lane. After a couple of hundred yards the lane bears right at the brow of the hill. Go through the gate here and follow the well-beaten path across the wide open field towards **West Charleton.** At the bottom of the field the path bears left beside the hedgebank on the right. Look out for a stile about 20 yards before the corner of the field. This leads across a stone bridge flanked by a pair of stiles. Climb up this last field, to the left of the duck pond to reach a stile at the top.

The walk beside **Frogmore Creek** provides a welcome window onto the charms of the drowned valleys of South Devon. Taste the water – it is undiluted sea; observe the bladderwrack attached to the rocks here. See the rocks themselves: slates at all angles, much interrupted with milkstone. Smell the sea air, look out across the water to lonely Ham Point opposite and more distant stretches of the creek and estuary beyond. It is a curious landscape: sea but not sea, land but not land, part of the friendly and intimate South Devon countryside and yet certainly unfrequented, indeed pretty inaccessible. Even in the late twentieth century these deep penetrating estuaries are ruled by the sea and by their abundant wildlife, and long may it remain so.

Charleton was once famous for its quarries. These were situated just beyond the point at which you turn back from Frogmore Creek. The slate dug here provided building stone for many churches in the South Hams, the collegiate chantry at Slapton and the square tower of Dartmouth Castle. Charleton quarry, unlike so many others in South Devon, thus served more than the needs of the immediate locality because its stone could easily be loaded onto boats and transported along the Kingsbridge estuary.

WALK 11   SLAPTON

via Slapton Ley

Map: South Devon Outdoor Leisure 20

Map Reference: 825447

Distance: 4½ miles

The footpath along the northern shore of Slapton Ley is an obvious choice for an unusual and attractive walk in South Devon. There is a choice of two ways by which you may quickly return to Slapton village which is itself a place of interest. The visit to the Ley is here extended by heading up the valley of the main stream entering the Ley and along a green lane to reach Pittaford. The route then bears back towards the village but here, unfortunately, there is no alternative but to use the road which is really only a quiet country lane, but straight, rather characterless and at least direct.

There is no car park in **Slapton**, but as the village is approached from the main road along Slapton Sands, there is a lay-by beside the road about half way up the hill and just before the Field Centre. Leave your car here and head back down the road (there is a path all the way down on the grass verge). Look out for the entrance to the **Nature Trail** on your right as you near the main road. This lakeside trail is well used, not least by people staying at the Field Centre, so is a clear and unmistakable way.

70

Beyond the end of the water you reach a junction of ways. You bear right to reach the Field Centre and the village via South Grounds. However, the route given here bears left to follow the duckboards across an expanse of boggy. ground. After this enjoyable section you reach another T-junction – bear right to head back to the village but left if you would rather complete the entire walk. This is an enclosed track between the base of a hill and a stream and can be deeply muddy. Follow the way until you reach the lane where you bear left and then very soon right, just before the bridge.

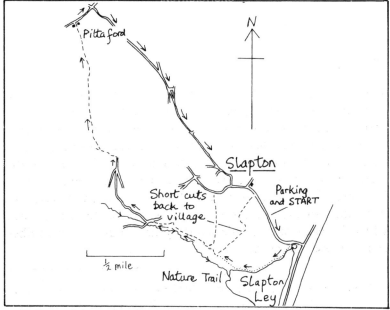

Follow this quiet lane at first further up the valley then bearing right up a smaller tributary combe. As the lane passes under the buildings on the bluff opposite notice the house on the right. A millstone leans against the wall beside the door and at the side of the house is an overshot water wheel in a good state of repair, even if the water no longer flows to turn the wheel. At the junction ahead carry straight on.

The lane soon swings to the left where it is signposted Public Bridleway. Pass the buildings on your left and follow the track uphill. This well-made way is mud-free and has a firm, stony base, so unlike the low-lying track followed last. An altitude of 400 feet giving wide views is achieved before reaching the farm buildings at **Pittaford**. Bear right at the lane and right again at the buildings in the dip ahead. Simply follow the lane, past the old school buildings at the junction back down into **Slapton** village.

Slapton is a particularly pleasant village, compact and situated near the head of a small valley. It is sufficiently elevated from the ley but not so much as to be exposed to the sea winds. Slapton lies on a local outcrop of red sandstone, a fact which is evidenced by the red soil in the fields surrounding the village. An hour or more can easily be spent exploring the village: its many quaint cottages with leaning chimneys, its church set squarely in the centre of the village and its two pubs, one tucked away below the overgrown tower which is all that remains of a medieval collegiate chantry.

This chantry was endowed in 1373 by Sir Guy de Brian; such institutions existed at least partly for the benefit of their founders; their incumbents undertaking to pray and hold masses for the sake of their benefactors' souls which to us may seem a curious understanding of Christianity. The chantries were abolished by Henry VIII, along with the monasteries, at the Dissolution in 1545.

The church has two capacious aisles making the overall proportions oddly broad and short. A booklet on sale inside serves as a comprehensive guide to the church, as well as providing information on the chantry and village. One remarkable piece of history was made when, in December 1943, the entire village was evacuated to make way for American troops who used Slapton Sands to practise manoeuvres in preparation for the Normandy landings. After D-Day, the village was left in peace and normal life was resumed once more.

Slapton Ley is the largest body of fresh water in the south west and, geologically speaking, is of very recent origin. Before the last glacial period, the hills behind the ley represented the old shore line. Sea level dropped during glaciation and rose again as the ice began to melt. This caused a shingle bank to be pushed landward; it probably began at the north end and extended southward with the southerly drift of the tide in Start Bay. Old maps of the area show the Gara and Start streams, which flow into the Upper and Lower Leys respectively, discharging directly into the sea, the Gara maintaining quite a wide estuary. These channels were eventually sealed; now the Upper Ley is a marsh while the Lower Ley decants into the sea by means of a culvert at Torcross.

Visitors to Slapton Ley Field Studies Centre are generally met on the course of the above ramble; the centre sells an inexpensive booklet entitled, *A Naturalist's Introduction to Slapton Ley Nature Reserve* which gives information on the wide variety of habitats and corresponding fauna and flora to be found here. These include the shingle ridge, which has different characteristics on its seaward and landward flanks, whilst the ley has reed beds, marshes and woodland.

Stone steps in wall

WALK 12   MALBOROUGH

via Batson, Salcombe, and North Sands

Map: South Devon Outdoor Leisure 20

Map Reference: 709398

Distance: 6 miles

Malborough occupies a commanding position atop that wedge of
the South Hams between the Kingsbridge Estuary to the east and
the estuary of the River Avon to the west. This large village and
important local crossroads stands upon a ridge of land around
the 350 feet contour and the piercing spire of its church is visible
for miles around.

The route described here includes an interesting mixture of
field paths, unmade tracks, woodland walks and quiet lanes; the
boating centre of Salcombe is the obvious half way stage. The sea
shore is reached at North Sands below the ruins of Salcombe
Castle. There are fine views from a hill-top before the descent to
Batson Creek. A saunter through the residential streets of
Salcombe could be exchanged for an exploration of the quays
beside the estuary but the higher road, described here, leads to a
most pleasant walk through a strip of woodland with delightful
views through the branches and across the estuary (whose waters
are strikingly blue even in winter) to the sand-fringed shores
opposite. The last leg from North Sands to Malborough takes
you first along a wooded path and then by an unspoilt valley.

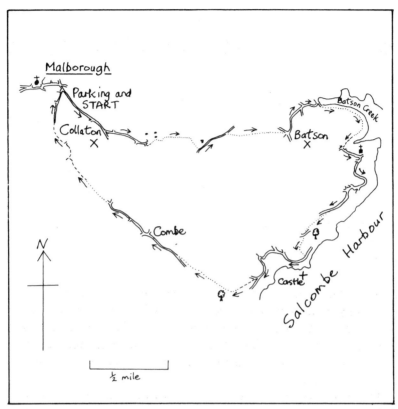

From Kingsbridge head over the crossroads in Malborough by **Salcombe Road Garage** to find the free car park situated in the wedge of land between Collaton Road and Salcombe Road. From the car park proceed downhill, away from Malborough, towards **Collaton Cross;** here bear left. Where the lane forks, bear left to **Collaton** (not right to Lower Collaton). Look out for a Public Footpath sign pointing down a rocky track to the right. Take this track above the farm buildings first bearing right, then left towards a gate which takes you into a field. Follow the hedgebank on the left to a stile in the bottom left corner. Step over the stream to the enclosed path which leads to a small field below some farm buildings and head for the stile on the far side.

Climb over the stile and turn left up the enclosed path to reach the lane at the entrance drive to the farm. Follow the lane uphill and look out for a Public Footpath sign on the right hand side. Climb the stile here to enter a field. Cross this field diagonally to reach a step stile. Head across the following field to a high point and a stile beside a gate – this is the most leftward of the three gates in front of you. Now follow the field boundary on the right towards a slab stile in the far right corner. Cross the centre of the next field to reach the Malborough-Salcombe road at **Batson Cross.**

Cross the main road and follow the lane down to Batson. Just as you reach Batson Creek you will spot a Public Footpath sign on the right. At the time of writing this right of way is blocked by an official sign indicating a diversion via the metalled road below. The cause of the diversion becomes evident in the form of a section of the path which had given way and collapsed into the road. The path soon reasserts itself, however, access to a Public Footpath being indicated about 50 yards further on. This leads you up to a kissing gate where you follow the way beside fields on the right with views through the trees above the creek to the left.

Three more fine wrought-iron kissing gates lead you to a more open section of the path with views down to the many yachts moored along Salcombe's quays. The path curves to the right towards a gas holder and a wooden gate. Walk past some cottages and at the road bear left towards the church; at the end of **Shadycombe Road** bear right. Soon you reach a patch of green provided with some benches and a great view up the Kingsbridge Estuary – an excellent spot to rest.

There are various ways of walking through the hillside town of **Salcombe** – the lower ways will take you to the quays and the town's pubs and shops. The way described here follows the road by the **Chalborough House Hotel** which you follow for some distance until you reach a signposted Public Footpath indicating a footpath through an area of woodland on the Salcombe hillside which makes a welcome change to suburban Salcombe. This path crosses a road before descending steeply to exit onto the road above **Salcombe Castle,** so well-placed to defend the entrance to the estuary. Bear right here and follow the road to **North Sands** where refreshment may be had (in season) at the Winking Prawn.

Follow the road via a hairpin bend to climb the hill which divides North and South Sands. On the crest of the hill bear right by the postbox in the wall along the lane signposted to **Malborough** and Kingsbridge. Bear sharp left along an unmade road; do not bear left again into De Courcy Road but carry on until the track reverts into a footpath through woods. Follow this path for some distance until you drop down to the lane.

At **Combe** take the right fork. Just past the next settlement do not follow the lane to the right but look out for the indicated Public Footpath sign to enter the field on the left. Follow the hedgebank on the right up a lovely green combe, enjoyment of which is later somewhat marred by the appearance of a small sewage works which serves Malborough. At this point the path becomes a track to reach a metalled lane at the house and farm ahead. Follow the lane to the right. Soon the lane takes a turn to the right but here follow the right of way straight ahead by a good footpath between hedgebanks. **Malborough Church** spire lies straight ahead and your road will lead you to the village crossroads and car park.

Malborough: Its prominent position on a high point and at the junction of a number of thoroughfares, including the Kingsbridge/Salcombe road, gives Malborough the impression of being larger than it is. All Saints Church boasts a broach spire which is a veritable landmark for miles around, even more so as it seems to denote the centre of this outlier of the South Hams between the Salcombe Estuary and the River Avon. The church is approached by a two storeyed porch; inside, the prospect, thanks to the Victorian restorers, is one of a long and rather bare nave – 'somewhat chilly', according to Pevsner, or, 'like a railway shed', according to Baring-Gould.

Salcombe, being well-sheltered by Bolt Head from the prevailing south-westerlies, provides a perfect harbour for smaller craft. Shipbuilding was once an important industry and reached its height in mid-Victorian times; fruit clippers designed to bring perishable cargoes at speed from exotic places were Salcombe's speciality. Fishing still provides a living for some Salcombe folk but, according to one contemporary account (*South Devon*, 1983), crabs and lobsters are being over-exploited and the size and quantity of the catch is consequently declining. An interesting presentation of Salcombe's maritime history may be seen at the town's own Maritime Museum which can be found above an old boathouse on Island Quay. A very interesting account of Salcombe's maritime history is given in the book *Devon Harbours;* the authors write that

> The main industry was undoubtedly shipbuilding and ship repairing. Four yards, employing over two hundred men, built vessels of every type from 40-ton smacks to 700-ton barques. In the space of fifty years as many as three hundred ships were launched; but losses were heavy, and it seems doubtful if more than a hundred Salcombe ships were ever in commission at the same time. Which was just as well perhaps, for the yards had to work at full capacity (a sixty-three hour week for an eighteen shillings wage) to keep even one hundred ships and their tackle in good repair.

Visitors have been coming to enjoy Salcombe's special charms since the eighteenth century. With the demise of shipbuilding, according to Black's *Guide to Devonshire* published at the turn of the century, Salcombe 'begins to turn its attention in earnest to visitors, claiming due rights as the most southerly and one of the most beautiful resorts of Devon, which has been kept back by want of communications, but might become a second Torquay if the railway could be pushed on to it.' The railway never did arrive and, if it had, would certainly by now have been long abandoned. There is, however, a good deal of twentieth century residential development, and the town and harbour prospers as a yachting centre.

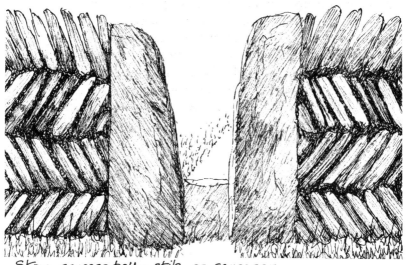

Stone squeeze belly stile or squeezer

WALK 13   **KINGSTON**

via St Ann's Chapel, Bigbury and Ringmore

Map: Bigbury Sheet SX 64

Map Reference: 635478

Distance: 6 miles (or may be shortened to 4½ miles)

This rather longer-than-average walk follows an enjoyable succession of footpaths, green roads and quiet lanes to complete a circuit of four villages, or three villages and a hamlet. Kingston, Bigbury and Ringmore all have their churches but St Ann's Chapel, notwithstanding its name, has neither church nor chapel extant, though all possess a pub. Ringmore and Kingston are particularly attractive settlements and there is always satisfaction in leaving one village and entering another by footpath across fields. Kingston is chosen as the starting point simply because there is some opportunity of parking your car here – in the road outside the church at the far west end of the village.

The route of this walk can quite easily be shortened to 4½ miles by heading due south at Marwell Cross (654473) to Ringmore, thus eliminating St Ann's Chapel and Bigbury.

From **Kingston church**, head past the Dolphin pub, a pleasing group of buildings occupying both sides of the narrow way; their situation explains the puzzling sign at the road below: 'Please drive slowly through the pub'. Bear left at the road and walk up through the village, then right at the T-junction and sharp left at the lane.

After about half a mile turn right towards the buildings of **South Langston**. (It is possible to cut a corner here by taking the signposted field path which leaves the lane from Kingston and heads directly across the open field to South Langston. The last time I walked here the field was planted with potatoes; the ridge and furrow being against the line of the path, making walking difficult).

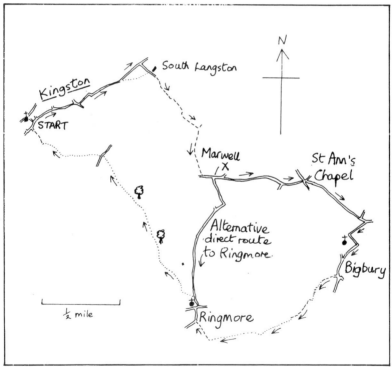

Follow the track through the farm buildings and on to reach a T-junction – the tower of Bigbury Church can be seen in the distance. Here turn right to reach a metalled lane. Bear left, past **Marwell Cross** and on to the junction at **St Ann's Chapel**.

The 1:25,000 map indicates these words in Gothic script and, upon enquiry, I was told that remains of an old chapel are incorporated into the fabric of the pub called the Pickwick, at the crossroads. Opposite the pub, behind the White House, is a private house called the Old Chapel, apparently a converted chapel of no great antiquity.

Cross the road and follow the lane opposite, past **Bigbury Parish Memorial Hall**. At the second small junction turn sharp right towards **Bigbury Church**, a large Victorian rebuilding, standing in an extensive churchyard and close by Bigbury Court. Follow the lane down towards the main road. The entrance to the Court reveals a notice which indicates that this plain, slate-hung house is an hotel. Observe, too, the large, circular, stone dovecote in the grounds.

Past the **Royal Oak** pub bear right by Bigbury Green along the signposted Public Footpath beside **Glen Cottage**. The way becomes very sunken and arched over with trees. At the bottom the way rises to a stile on the left. Cross here and follow the gappy hedgerow on your right downhill. At the foot cross over a dilapidated stone wall and shortly reach a stile which drops you into a sunken (and usually boggy) green lane. Bear right and follow the way as it turns to the left.

Eventually you reach a steel gate – go through and bear right to follow the open track to a footbridge over a stream. Here you will spot a yellow arrow indicating the right of way crossing the field to the left towards a pair of railway sleeper gateposts. From here follow the arrow to a stile in the top corner of the field. You can see down the valley to the sea at Challaborough and Burgh Island. Cross the stile and follow the lane to **Ringmore**.

Turn right at **Rock Cottage**, past the village stores and on to the church. The pub is down the lane to the left of the church and not directly on our route.

With your back to **Ringmore church** turn left and sharp left again. Just past the manor look out for a gap in the stone wall, indicating a Public Footpath by a kissing gate. Cross the field diagonally to reach an iron gate; follow the path between the hedge and wall to the gateposts ahead.

The way from here to Kingston is relatively complicated but, thankfully, every junction is marked by the friendly yellow arrow to indicate the existence and the direction of the right of way.

You can see the singular-looking pile of Oldcastle to the right, with its gothicised bay window and castellated tower. Head for the left corner of the field and then look out for a stile in the fence about 20 yards ahead on the left. Cross here and descend to the valley bottom. Cross the step stile and follow the beaten path through the trees, then through a gate beside a ruined cottage. Follow the brook upstream over a meadow which in early summer is full of yellow iris.

Another stile and more yellow arrows lead you ahead by an enclosed path which eventually begins to rise through the woods to emerge at a field. Bear right along the field edge following the boundary as it swings to the left by some abandoned cars.

Look out for a stile in the corner where the track bears left. Cross the next field, as indicated, to a stile. You can see **Kingston** ahead. Bear left here along the lane, then after a few yards cross the stile on your right. Follow the right hand boundary, cross the stile in the top corner, then at the next corner follow the hedge on the right. At the bottom corner there is a stile on the right. Cross and follow the bottom of the field to the far corner where you will find an old stone slab stile. Cross here towards the cottage and bear right to reach the lane into Kingston.

The villages of **Kingston, Bigbury** and **Ringmore** and the hamlet of **St Ann's Chapel** all have their interest and attractions. Ringmore has perhaps the most favourable position with its view southwards to the little cove at Challaborough – a prospect seen to advantage from beneath the tower of the early medieval parish church of All Saints.

During the Civil War the rector here was the Rev. William Lane, a devout royalist and one whose Christian principles did not extend to a refusal to take up arms. Indeed, together with some men from his parish, he defended the bridge across the Avon at Aveton Gifford against the Parliamentarians and was highly successful in destroying convoys of food and ammunition. Eventually, reinforcements were called for from Plymouth – several boatloads of soldiers landed at Ayrmer Cove (just west of Challaborough) and advanced on Kingston, seeking revenge on the rector. William Lane was forewarned and took refuge in a little room in the church tower. His house was ransacked but the rector himself escaped detection by holing up in the tower for three months, secretly supplied with food by members of his flock. He eventually escaped to France.

The village pub is found down the lane below the church and is known as Journey's End though it is not, perhaps sadly, at the end of this ramble.

St Lawrence Church at Bigbury is of somewhat larger proportions than those at the other villages. Of the main fabric, the tower alone survives; the remainder was rebuilt in the 1870s.

The chapel at St Ann's Chapel is in fact incorporated into the pub at the crossroads called the Pickwick Inn. This piece of information was imparted to me by someone in a neighbouring garden. Anne Born in her recent book *South Devon* says that an underground stream flows through the pub's cellar and that the chapel may have been built on the site of the pagan Saint Ann, famed for eating babies and discarding their bones into wells – another of those shadowy Celtic saints with a most extraordinary claim to saintliness!

WALK 14   MODBURY

via Aylestone Brook

Map: Ivybridge Sheet SX 65/75

Map Reference: 658515

Distance: 2½ miles

The small and ancient town of Modbury is, on most sides, surrounded by higher land. The Aylestone Brook flows through and beneath the town from the north-east. This short but enjoyable ramble begins by tracing the brook out of the town through a gap in the hills on the south side. In the valley below the brook takes the grain of the land in a westerly, then south-westerly, direction to join the River Erme a couple of miles from its mouth.

The route of this walk follows field paths to reach a lane leading south, then an old hedged track which starts on a hill top above the valley but eventually leads to the valley bottom where a field path is followed upstream towards the unusual spire of Modbury church.

Leave the main car park to the south of **Modbury's** main street by a gate in its far corner. The path leads you beside the brook and meadow; to the right a steep slope reaches up to Modbury Church which, like a castle, stands sentinel above the town. Follow the way past the **Old Mill** on the right to reach a slab stile. You may notice an interesting cut incorporating a miniature bridge which gives direct access from the mill to the road above.

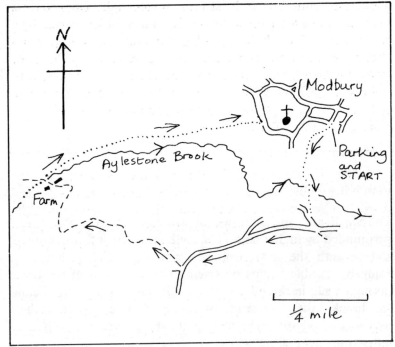

Cross the stile and walk down to the bridge across the mill leat and on across and up the field towards a slab stile in the hedgerow opposite marked by a Public Footpath sign. Bear left to join the lane above and then turn sharp right. From this lane you can enjoy views back over Modbury and towards Dartmoor beyond. Follow this lane to the top of the hill and a signposted drive to Butland. Do not take this metalled track but instead follow the unmade track between hedges immediately to the right. At first this is pretty much a sunken lane and little is visible except through the occasional field-gate. Further on, where the path descends the hillside, the view opens out, and you can see southwards along the Erme valley.

Follow the track down through the farm buildings, over the bridge across the brook and climb the stile signposted Public Footpath just on the right. Now head straight up the valley towards the church with the stream on your right. Go through a steel gate and eventually leave the fields in a far left corner by a gate to enter a lane. Follow this lane for a few yards, step over a stream and climb the stile on the right to re-enter a field. Now follow the hedgerow on the left up the slope, across a stile, until you reach a gate which drops you into the lane. Turn right here and bear left through the churchyard and on to reach the road leading down through Modbury.

Modbury certainly has the feel of a town about it but one cannot help musing that here is a place that has seen better and more stirring times. Its main street has some handsome little town houses, some of which exhibit slate-hanging, like many buildings in Totnes. Modbury had borough status from the mid-twelfth century, holding a weekly market and an annual nine-day fair.

St George's Church has an unusual medieval spire still intact and is an attractive building generally, well worth exploring. The Champernowne Chapel contains many effigies of former lords of the manor. Sir Richard Champernowne kept a company of musicians which, their fame spreading, were summoned to Windsor by Henry VIII. Sir Richard paid for new costumes but, at Court they were ignored and dismissed, poor Champernowne having to pay all the expenses involved. Later, Elizabeth I summoned the bard but was answered by Sir Richard that the last encounter had all but bankrupted him. The Queen responded by confiscating many of his properties. The Champernownes nevertheless remained loyal to the crown and took up arms against the Parliamentarians in the Civil War. During the battle of 1642 the Roundheads burnt the Manor House, only one wing of which remains today, close by the church.

WALK 15   ERMINGTON

via Sequers Bridge and the River Erme

Map: Ivybridge Sheet SX 65/75

Map Reference: 637531

Distance: 2½ miles

This is a short ramble from an attractive village situated about a
mile from the A379 Modbury-Plymouth road. A riverside walk
is followed by field paths which follow a slightly elevated course
back up the quiet and unspoilt Erme valley with views northwards to Dartmoor. Unfortunately, there are no rights of way on
either side of the beautiful Erme valley and estuary below
Sequer's Bridge, although the gardens at Flete House are open
to the public and special permission to explore further may be
sought.

There is a limited amount of space for car parking at the
village crossroads below the Crooked Spire pub.

Start the walk in **Ermington** by heading down **Town Hill**
towards the road below. Follow the road for a short distance but
look out for a stile and Public Footpath sign opposite **Ermewood
House** . Follow the right of way by keeping fairly close to the
bank (although this does not entail tracing the river's every bend
and loop). Head straight on until you approach **Sequer's Bridge**

and climb up to the road by a stile on the right. The entrance to the grounds of Flete House is marked by a gatehouse and the start of a drive through the grounds on the far side.

Cross the bridge and immediately bear left down some steps into the field below the road. Head diagonally across this field to reach a gate in the opposite corner. Follow the track to the left, through the farm buildings. The last of these buildings is an old stone barn; here you take the track to the right of the barn heading slightly uphill; the spire of Ermington church now comes back into view.

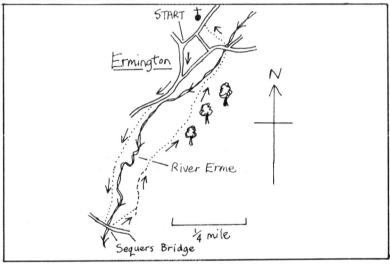

Take a left fork along a well-marked track between a hedge on the left and a barbed wire fence on the right. Follow the left hand hedge until you reach a gate in the far left hand corner of the field. The right of way is here indicated by a yellow arrow. Enter the field and follow the beaten path diagonally across and down to the far left hand corner, at the edge of the wood. With hanging woods on the hillside to your right and views beyond to the Dartmoor hills with, closer at hand, the village of Ermington spread beneath the allegedly crooked spire of its church, here is a prospect you may wish to contemplate for some time.

At the bottom corner you climb a step-stile to head in the same direction across the next field towards the river. Now follow the river bank upstream through a couple of gates towards the farm buildings ahead. Look out for a yellow arrow at the barn indicating the right of way behind the remaining buildings, thus avoiding the farm yard, and sticking close by the river bank. You quickly emerge onto the road by a stone slab stile. Bear left. You may notice an old milestone here indicating 11 miles to both Plymouth and Totnes.

Cross the road and the bridge and make for a gap in the wall which leads you across playing fields towards the **church**. Leave the church by the gate on the south side and follow the beaten path by the kissing gate and a couple of benches across the green. This leads you to the little square in front of the Crooked Spire pub.

Ermington is an attractive place, sufficiently removed and elevated from the main road to free it from through traffic and give it a view down and across the valley to the hanging wood on the far side. The village pub, the Crooked Spire, is named after a peculiar feature of the church. The famous spire is said by some to have been built by a bowlegged mason with a squint – no doubt a member of an abused medieval minority group whose work has nevertheless stood the test of time. Another 'explanation' has it that the spire of the church got the crick in its neck through looking down to see a sixteenth century bride enter the building in her bridal dress, yet another is that the lean or twist in the spire was caused by its being struck by lightning.

The Church of St Peter and St Paul is large and impressive from any viewpoint and stands slightly apart from the village. If approached via the unusual Italianate lychgate, as it is on this ramble, you perhaps have an expectation that the interior will be somewhat out of the ordinary too. You will not be disappointed, for inside is an abundance, a veritable feast, of superb woodcarving. This is the work of Violet Pinwill and her sisters, daughters of a former rector here. Their work decorates altar rails, the reredos, the pulpit, bench-ends, the font cover, side screens and the beams and bosses in the chancel roof. The detail of the carving is well worth inspection: a host of wild creatures, many of them such as one might find in the Devon countryside, accompany figures of more heavenly origin.

Wooden squeezer with step

FURTHER READING

BARING-GOULD, Sabine
Devon, Methuen, 1907

BORN, Anne
A History of Kingsbridge and Salcombe, Phillimore, 1986
South Devon, Gollancz, 1983

BOYLE, Vernon C. and PAYNE, Donald
Devon Harbours, Christopher Johnson, 1952

DURRANCE, E.M. and LAMING, D.J.C., eds.
The Geology of Devon, University of Exeter, 1982

HEMERY, Eric
Historic Dart, David and Charles, 1982

HOSKINS, W.G.
Devon, David and Charles, new ed. 1972

MANNING-SANDERS, Ruth
The River Dart, Westaway Books, 1951

MEE, Arthur, ed.
The King's England: Devon, Hodder and Stoughton, 1938

PEVSNER, Nikolaus
The Buildings of England: South Devon, Penguin, 1952

ST LEGER-GORDON, D.
Devonshire, Hale, 1950

SEYMOUR, Deryck and HAZZARD, Jack
Berry Pomeroy Castle, Published by the authors, 1982

STANES, Robin
A Fortunate Place: the history of Slapton in South Devon, Field
Studies Council, 1983

WILLIAMS, Ken and REYNOLDS, Dermot
The Kingsbridge Branch, Oxford Publishing Company, 1977

WILLY, Margaret
The South Hams, Hale, 1955

TALL SHIPS IN TORBAY
John Pike

In this book are the stirring events of history: the defeat of the Spanish Armada, the capture of Napoleon and the landing of William, Prince of Orange. Here too are the less familiar episodes: ruthless pirates and their struggles against the Revenue men, the press gangs which terrorised the male population, the provision of support services for the British Fleet anchored in the Bay, local shipbuilding, emigration to the Colonies, the development of the Coastguard Service and the modern fishing industry, and much more.

Tall Ships in Torbay is expertly researched and well documented; it is also fully illustrated with an outstanding collection of pictures and will prove of lasting worth to anyone who knows Torbay or who has a fascination with things maritime.

144 pages; full colour cover; numerous illustrations and map
ISBN 0 948578 03 3   Price £4.95

The WALKER'S COMPANION
Edited and Introduced by Roger Jones
Illustrated by Edward Dowden

The works of some 23 writers, beginning with Wordsworth and ending with Henry Willaimson are quoted here and all illustrate some aspect of the walker's art. The urge to get away from it all and get close to nature opens us to the varied pleasures of walking: the pursuit of health, relaxation and renewal. All these are celebrated in prose and poetry. So too are the delights of the country footpath and mountain track, whether they be the fruits of a day's ramble or of an extended walking tour.

The West of England figures prominently in this anthology, in particular Wilkie Collins hiking through Cornwall and excerpts from two accounts of marathon walks undertaken in the last century: Walter White from London to Land's End in 1854 and the American Elihu Burritt walking between the same two points ten years later. The former trekked 425 miles during the month of August on a budget of £10. Both accounts are full of interest and some of the most entertaining and illuminating incidents are quoted in this absorbing collection.

'*This remarkable collection of prose and verse .... a charming ramble of a book*'   *Wiltshire Gazette and Herald*

112 pages; full colour cover; 17 pen and ink drawings
ISBN 0 9506563 5 6   Price £2.95

GREEN ROAD TO LAND'S END

Roger Jones

Illustrated by Edward Dowden

Journey's End

On May Day 1984 Roger Jones set out to fulfil a modest but long held ambition to walk from London to Land's End.

He soon discovered that the five or six mile rambles to which he was accustomed had not prepared him for the rigours of this long-distance walk. The first day's 26 miles left him not only footsore but almost unable to put one foot in front of the other.

After six days he arrived at Avebury in Wiltshire, called his wife and took two days rest at home in Bradford on Avon. One new pair of walking boots and a visit to the hospital later, he started out once more and happily completed his route to the far west of England.

The idea behind the walk was to link together the various bits of the West Country with which the author was familiar and to witness the gradual unfolding of the landscape at a mere walking pace. In doing so he developed an appreciation of proper boots and enjoyed an endlessly absorbing panorama in the glorious month of May.

200x128mm   144 pages   Full colour cover   17 pen and ink drawings
ISBN   0 948578 01 7   Price £2.95

A BOOK OF NEWTON ABBOT   Roger Jones

Newton Abbot is a town many people know for its race track, its weekly market, or as somewhere through which they pass on their way further west. The coming of the railway transformed the town. The weekly market has endured and the town continues to serve as an important commercial centre for South Devon and Dartmoor. Beneath and behind the Victorian and modern expansion and rebuilding of the town lies a history as long and fascinating as that of any Devon community.

Written by a former librarian of Newton Abbot, this is the third edition of a book which first appeared in 1979.

216x150mm   152 pages   Full colour cover   Numerous old photographs
ISBN 0 948578 06 8   Price £3.95